Working My Way Home

"This memoir by Catherine Naylor is a humorous, beautiful, poignant, remarkably sane and courageous story of a very difficult, and yet wondrous year she spent trying to find a home in an impossibly convoluted place—Taos (rhymes with chaos!), New Mexico. I read it in one sitting, swept along by much laughter and also a few tears. Almost every chapter on 'the art of survival' astonished me. Catherine took so many lickings, yet she kept on ticking! Her life journey during her first year in Taos reads like a kind of gentle Candide, with more pitfalls than you can possibly imagine. And yet they are all recounted with much insight, compassion, and lively humor that totally captured my heart as Catherine fell in love with her new home. I thank her from my captured heart for this wild odyssey. I wish she'd come back to Taos one day and sit down at Dori's Bakery and Café with me for a cup of coffee and a Hash Brown Heaven, so that we could reminisce about old times. Those were the days, my friend, and, like this book, they were a remarkable piece of work."

— John Nichols, author and activist

"In Taos at a time when the days passed by on the edges of the daily breeze and a lazy sun shone down on plucky pedestrians, Catherine Naylor captures the poetic moments of place and people in this working woman's memoir of the 70s. In effect, she recreates the resonance of the zeitgeist for today's lucky readers."

— Bill Whaley, *Horse Fly* Publisher and Editor, author of *Gringo Lessons*

"*Working My Way Home*, Catherine's book about her first year in Taos, is a tragi-comic tale of trying to make ends meet *aqui en* Taos, while learning the intricacies of the local culture(s), the subtle (and not so subtle) nuances of language and politics. Weaving a spell with poetry and prose, Catherine learns the code of the Taos road, along with learning to dig ditches and carry water, both literally and metaphorically. It is the universal story of all who come here and find themselves somehow welcomed by the Mountain, even as it brings one to ones's knees!"

— Lynne Robinson, writer, blogger of *Taos Style*

Working My Way Home
A Taos Story

*Set in the country town of
Taos, New Mexico,
where beauty, history and mystery
are equally and eternally intertwined.*

by
Catherine Naylor

Wink Books

Working My Way Home: A Taos Story. Copyright 2018 by Catherine Naylor. All rights reserved. Printed in the United States of America. No part of this book may be used or reproduced in any manner whatsoever without written permission, other than in the case of brief quotations embodied in critical articles and reviews. For information contact: Wink Books, P.O. Box 153, El Prado NM 87529, winkbooks.com

—

FIRST EDITION 2018

—

Library of Congress Catalog-in-Publication-Data

Working My Way Home: A Taos Story / Catherine Naylor – 1st ed.
Cover illustration by Briana Waltman
Illustration on page 15 by Nora Anthony
Edited by Dory Hulburt and Connie Josefs
Graphic design by Kelly Pasholk, Wink Visual Arts
Published by Wink Books

Library of Congress Control Number: 2018956431
ISBN: 978-0-9973950-4-4

Personal Memoir, Autobiography, Taos,
Wit and Humor, Coming of Age

*We are all wanderers on this earth.
Our hearts are full of wonder
and our souls are deep with dreams.*

— A GYPSY PROVERB

Mom, you always said,
"Cathy, you have a book in you."

Well, Mom,
Here's that book!

For my Mother,
Alice La Plant Naylor
1906 - 1996

Acknowledgments

My nephew Michael Golden was like the Town Crier, who announces that a great thing is coming, is almost here, is here! He believed in me, encouraged me, walked beside me and if he hadn't, there would be no book today.

Thanks to Kelly Pasholk of Wink Visual Arts for her beautiful design work. Kelly too walked beside me, many times holding my hand as a friend and co-worker.

Thanks to Dory Hulburt and Connie Josefs for their edits of this book. Where would we be without our editors?

Thanks to Bill Whaley for giving me the the opportunity to develop my writing skills for nine years at his Horse Fly newspaper. I still call him "Boss."

Thanks to every person whoever called Taos, New Mexico their home, if only for a day or for several years or for a lifetime. You have been my inspiration, my guides and companions in good times and hard.

— Catherine

Contents

Preface	1
Taos	2
1977: It Begins	3
Uno: The Front Desk Clerk	10
You Talkin' to Me?	15
Cañon	21
Dos: Newspaper Clerk	22
Joe García	26
Taos' Santa Fe Road	31
The Godfathers – Taos Style	33
Tres: The Housekeeper	35
Quatro: The Caregiver	38
Cinco: The Art Gallery Sitter	49
1978: It Continues	54
Seis: Front Desk Clerk – Again!	60
Siete: Substitute Teacher	68
Ocho: Substitute Teacher – Really	73
Nueve: The Hostess	81
Diez: Teacher – Almost!	87
Once: The Waitress	93
Doce: Office Manager	94
Trece: Gallery Sitter	97
Catorce: The Gardener	98
Quince: Kelly Girl	100
Dieciséis: The ESL Teacher	101
Diecisiete: Alcohol and Drug Counselor – Bingo!..	106
Dieciocho: Writer and Assistant Editor	114
Epilogue	115
About the Author	116

Preface

IN JUNE OF 1977, I stepped into an ancient conversation between the physical beauty of a high desert valley, encircled by mountains and crisscrossed by the green waters of acequias, and the psyche of that place, which had been shaped over a thousand years by the Taos Pueblo Native Americans.

Hikes in the mountains, picnics down by the river, cafés and coffee shops, the arts, the toughness of a frontier life, but mostly the people—my friends and neighbors, my fellow employees, and later my students, counseling clients and colleagues—all wove, thread by colorful thread, year after year, the patterned quilt of a life. My life.

Now, after thirty-seven years in Taos, New Mexico, where I never intended to stay when I was just passing through on a camping trip, I ask myself, "When did I know that Taos was home?" The natives know they are home for they've never left it. They know things that the outsider will never know, things buried so deep within the native psyche that they remain unknown to the outsider, the visitor, the wanderer.

My curiosity is with the outsider, being one myself. When do we make a place a home?

Did I make Taos my home the evening I crossed the Río Grande into Taos, New Mexico, or my first Christmas at the Pueblo with those huge medieval bonfires, or when I snagged my first good job?

Taos

I haven't been here long enough
to cut a path across a field
or make a friend.

I don't know what this land
will yield, nor what scars are still tender
in the memory of its people.

I don't know which villages along
the back roads will take me in.

I only know the hollyhocks and old adobes
haunt me and the mountains and blue mesas
hold me. The spirit of this place has entered me.

I will plant something here.

1977

It Begins

> *"Taos has always possessed the curious magic of seeming to be discovered by every person drawn into its mountain ringed beauty."*
>
> — FRANK WATERS 1902 - 1995

Louise White and I met in a women's writing group in Santa Cruz, California. Often after the writing group dispersed, Louise and I would sit under a tree and tell our stories to each other. We were amazed how alike we were. Both were curious and had taken trips outside of Illinois, both had stacks of books and journals, both had done our paternal and maternal genealogy, both had many friends.

One day, Louise placed a well underlined book into my hands, saying, "Here, learn the true history of our country. I'm enraged. I need someone to talk to about this."

I took Howard Zinn's *People's History of the United States, 1492 - Present* up to my cabin, settled on the front porch and started reading. It didn't take many pages for me to become enraged at my grammar and high school teachers who hadn't told me the truth about our country's systematic genocide of the Native Americans.

Soon I became enraged at myself. Why hadn't I discovered the facts? How could I have lived in the world close to forty years and not known this? What else didn't I know?

After much discussion, Louise and I made plans for a summer camping trip to visit as many Native American homelands as we could, seeing with our own eyes at least a glimpse of their world. I fueled my anger into hours spent at the Santa Cruz public library doing research for the trip and making a tentative itinerary through Havasupai, Navajo, Hopi and Pueblo homelands. When I discovered there were nineteen surviving Pueblos, from some seventy-one in the 1600s, up and down the Río Grande in New Mexico and that the Taos Pueblo in the north was considered the most traditional, I made Taos our eastern most point. Back then I believed in plans. Besides, Claire Morrill's *A Taos Mosaic* dropped from a library shelf onto my foot. I know—hard to believe. Believe it.

When school was over and Louise and I were free, we started out for Arizona in my red Toyota Corolla, with our camping gear, a big cooler, our duffle bags, tent, maps, journals and books in the hatchback.

After months of traveling through the Southwest, camping on Native American homelands, climbing the cliff dwelling ruins, and visiting old Spanish villages, we camped near Hopewell Lake, a scant fifty miles from Taos Pueblo, which was going to be our last stop before returning home to Santa Cruz.

This small, sweet lake with only a handful of people and a couple of dogs was exactly what we needed. The trip had bent our minds and put over a thousand miles on the car. We thought the summer could hold no more magic. We called it a day and set up camp. We stretched, ate, went over the highlights and lowlights of the trip thus far, and went to bed early.

The next morning I told Louise I would love a full day and another night at the lake before we took on Taos, which from my readings seemed to be a complex place. She agreed. We cleaned out the car, sorted what we had collected, and enjoyed being off wheels and on our feet. That day we decided to change our names. We'd be Louisa and Catherine. Approaching forty, I felt it was time to give up the diminutive Cathy. Louise just plain loved all things Southern. So another day of loafing, watching people fish from their canoes, just being and enjoying beauty.

The next morning, Louisa said, "Let's go to Taos."

But I wasn't ready and asked for another day. I wasn't ready yet to leave for I felt something powerful was going to happen and I needed to ready myself. If nothing else, I needed more solitude, more centering.

On the third day, Louisa said, "Today we go."

After reaching Taos, we drove a few miles up Taos Canyon to set up camp, listening to beautiful music along the way. We planned to visit the Taos Pueblo in the morning. After our camp was set up we drove back to Taos Plaza in search of celebratory margaritas to celebrate my June 14th fortieth birthday. I parked near a fellow leaning against a post in front of the Río Grande Rexall Drugstore.

"Wait here," I told Louise. "I'll ask him where that music we've been hearing is coming from."

As I walked toward him, we looked straight at each other.

He had high cheekbones and wide-spaced black eyes; long silky black hair pulled back in a ponytail; a black western hat with a silver band; jeans and a belt with a round, silver, turquoise-studded buckle. His tan western leather boots were scuffed and turned up at the toes.

"Excuse me," I said. "I'm wondering where that music is coming from?"

Without changing his comfortable slouch, he looked over to the main street and lifting his chin slightly, said, "Go south down that street a couple of blocks to the Indian Hills Inn on your left. I think you'll find what you're looking for."

I thanked him. He tipped his head. Walking back to the car, I wondered if he knew something that I didn't know. I wasn't looking for anything. I just wanted to have a good time.

What I was beginning to know was that this was a place that could enchant me, which, perhaps, already had.

I beckoned to Louise to get out of the car. I told her that he had said that we could walk to where the music is.

"What's the name of this town anyway?" she asked.

"It's spelled TAOS. Beats me how to pronounce it. Anyway, we're just passing through."

When we got to the Indian Hills Inn, we couldn't find the lounge. We circled back to the front desk to inquire about it and encountered an unhappy-looking portly older gentleman chomping on a smelly cigar and thumbing through a pile of magazines.

"Excuse me, Sir," I said. "I think we're lost."

"So where do you want to be?"

"We want to find the lounge where the music is."

"Go down that hallway over there. You'll walk right into it. By the way," he said, chomping on his smelly cigar, "my front desk clerk took off yesterday without notice to go back to her home in Port Angeles, Washington. Do either of you need a job?"

"I do."

I couldn't believe those words popped out of my mouth.

"Good," the manager said. "Start tomorrow."

"But I'm camping up in the canyon. I'll need a few days to find a rental. You know ... with a shower and stuff." It was as if I were standing outside of myself, incredulously watching this exchange with no power to stop it. Louise was pulling at the cuff of my jacket.

He swiveled around, took a key off a brown corkboard behind him and handed it to me. "Room three. Use it 'til you get a rental. Start tomorrow. Two o'clock sharp."

Huh? No form to fill out? No interview? No résumé nor references to check? I thought we might have taken a wrong turn and weren't in America anymore.

Louise and I stepped outside, but the fresh air didn't clear my foggy mind.

"Catherine! What in the world was that all about?"

"I don't know."

"What do you mean you don't know? How am I getting home? It's your car!"

"I don't know … I just have to stay … just for the summer. My new job in Santa Cruz doesn't start until September. I did notice a Greyhound Bus schedule at the front desk."

Louise was in a huff, giving me the cold shoulder. We decided to give those celebratory margaritas a miss and went back up Taos Canyon, broke camp, drove back to the Inn and settled into room three. The rhythm of the car rolling along the roads had gotten into my bones and had lulled me to sleep each night in our tent, but in my motel twin bed, which must have been just a stone's throw from the lounge, I was tossed in a little rowboat on the high seas of rock and roll. The lyrics were mostly in Spanish.

"Exactly where are we?" I called over to Louise.

"Beats me. You made out the itinerary."

"Did I really take a job here?"

"Well, we're sleeping in room three!" She mumbled. "Geez! I can't believe it."

La Bamba finally rocked me to sleep.

UNO

The Front Desk Clerk

The next morning, Louisa lightened up with the help of a breakfast of bacon and eggs, toast and coffee in the motel's lounge. It began to sink in that we had arrived in a new town and landed a free hotel room, a shower, color TV, a swimming pool and restaurant. That first week I worked and Louise toured the little town.

I learned how to sell motel rooms, tell tourists what to see in a town I hadn't seen myself, process credit cards, tally up and, if I were lucky, balance the day's take, while, when necessary, finessing the complaints.

"We can't get this damn television to work!"

"Back in Louisville we could bring our motorcycles and dogs in. What's this, the Ritz?"

"Excuse me, Miss, but there's a snake in the tub."

My stock response was "I'm sorry. I'll call the manager." His stock response over the phone was "Oh, shit!" Nothing was ever done. Most of the complainers left and the desperate ones at two o'clock in the morning just dealt with the inconveniences and never said another word.

My fellow employees were proud to claim, "I'm from Taos!" The rest of us were forced to own up to

Chicago, L.A., Brooklyn or some other godforsaken place. Sometimes I got the sense that to be born outside of Taos County was seen as a grave misfortune.

I will always be grateful to Lisa Quintana, Kathy Martínez, Juanita Sánchez and Flora Tafoya, who never seemed to notice that my skin was whiter than a summer cloud. From them I began to feel welcomed. They informed me that if I carried my weight the people would open up to me, but since I was Anglo, and fair-haired at that, it might take me a bit longer.

In those early years, like most Anglos, I received the run-of-the-mill epithets—güera, gringa, and palomino because of a blond streak in my Irish, early onset, silver-white hair. But I took the name-calling in stride, thinking it was a good experience to live as a minority. But one day I received a most splendid insult! It took my breath away and set bells off in my heart. All I remember is the word and how it set me free. I don't remember the circumstances nor who uttered the word, thinking it would put me in my place—which thankfully it did.

"You're an outsider!"

Omigod! Someone knew the truth about me and uttered it publicly! What a relief! I've been outed. The inside and outside have been matched up and I had become visible. I could be myself! It was an absolute thrill. I was a Gypsy come home!

My fellow employees took pity on me. They taught me the motel business, ran interference for me, laughed with me, ate with me and generally showed me how things were done in Taos, which included teaching me Spanish swear words.

I met the tourists. The largest group was from Texas, the second largest from Oklahoma. The rest came from throughout the States and around the world. Some came to see the Taos Pueblo, some to buy art, some to check out the ski resort for winter. Most conversations were an exciting sharing of where we'd been, why we travel, impressions of our hometowns and now of Taos. To others I was "honey," who would change a hundred dollar bill so they could pick up the fifteen-cent *Denver Post*.

After my first week it was time for Louisa to board the Greyhound and head home, after enjoying what she said was the best vacation she'd ever had. I told her I'd see her and the writing group at summer's end back in Santa Cruz.

By week two at the Indian Hills, the fellows of La Raza began to stop by the front desk to check out the new gal before she too disappeared like the last one. They informed me that they were Chicanos and after a few conversations they began dropping off books for me to read to save me from my ignorance. The first book to plop on the desk was Rudolfo Anaya's *Bless Me, Ultima*. Next was a mimeographed and much-folded copy of Rodolfo Corky Gonzales' epic poem *Yo Soy Joaquín*. Then came Stan Steiner's *La Raza: The*

Mexican Americans and *The Vanishing White Man*. My first weekend trip was to the courthouse in Tierra Amarilla, some eighty miles northwest of Taos, where land grant activist Reies López Tijerina's 1967 armed raid took place in the court house. Tijerina led the fight to take back land confiscated by an Anglo surveyor during the mid 1960s.

In the evenings the locals gathered to enjoy a good time in the lounge, shooting pool and rocking to the loudest Spanish music in the valley—Jesse Candelaria (aka Freddy Fender), brothers Johnny and Billy Archuleta, Nick Branchal, the Kardoriffic Rock Band, Ruben Niter Martínez and his brother Fito of the Latin Express, and Vito y Alan. Susie Trujillo and Beto Pacheco tended bar; Gilbert Tollardo guarded the doors.

Every couple of nights, fistfights erupted and the place went wild. I got the feeling sometimes that I had taken a wrong turn and landed across the border and I was nervous about being the informant who called the Federales, having neither passport nor green card.

"Officer Rivera? Hi, it's me again. Blood and guts tonight. A woman was dancing with her boyfriend when her husband walked in. Chairs and glass are flying all over the place."

"Officer Trujillo? Hey, Manny, how's it going? Look, the Mountain Rats just roared in on their motorcycles. Can you cruise by every ten minutes? Yeah, I know you've got your hands full with Los Compadres, but we're going to top them tonight."

"Hey, Chief Lucero, something different! Five guys naked in the swimming pool. Doing a lot of diving from the high board. Can you get them out? The floating tequila bottles, too."

"Gallegos? Look, those dudes are back. Won't let anyone in unless they pay a fifty-cent protection fee. No one's complaining except the manager."

Yes, the lounge drew the rambunctious crowd that summer and I was sweating the fights, dealing with the cops, sweeping up the broken glass, rushing back to the front desk to book in more lost gringos, without a moment to wonder where I was, what in the world I was doing, or what my mother would think.

One day the manager told me I was a great front desk clerk but he had to let me go. He refused to give a reason. Word was it was an order from his wife. I would soon learn that Taos was not a union town and workers had no rights.

I had lasted six weeks. But I didn't leave empty-handed. I took with me my first impressions of Taos, new friends, great books and music, like *Allá en el Rancho Grande, Cielito Lindo*, and, of course, *La Bamba*.

Years later, when I felt at home and was working at Taos's popular monthly newspaper, *Horse Fly*, I memorialized those conversations with La Raza in the following column.

You Talkin' to Me?
June 15, 2005

I've been called a lot of things in my life, but the worst happened right here in Taos. It happened when I was newly arrived, a fragile moment for any immigrant, especially a minority. I remember it well. I was at La Cocina enjoying the conviviality of happy hour. In the '70s, as you will recall, we all got new labels: Chicano, Feminist, Gay, Black, etc. And that early summer evening, I was about to get my new label that would set me back on my sandaled heels, calling out to Ruthie for another Tecate with a lime, please. The local color I was talking with was setting me straight about La Raza and how things were going to be in northern New Mexico from then on out. He kept emphasizing his point by prefacing his theories, stories, and predictions with "You Anglos."

Now for me, Anglo meant anything or anyone having to do with England. I kept looking over my shoulder to see who the heck he was talking to. Certainly not me. I was a descendant of the Irish who had suffered mightily at the hands of the English and who never missed an opportunity to take a swipe at anything Anglo.

Finally, I asked the "Chicano" who he was calling "Anglo."

"You!" he said.

"Me? You're calling me Anglo?" I was flabbergasted. My Leahy, Daley, Murphy ancestors would punch him out if they could once again gather in a pub.

"I'm not Anglo!" I cried, hanging my head and running my fingers through my hair. "Call me white, call me a gringa, call me American, call me Irish American, but for God's sake, don't call me Anglo."

Our roles switched and I became the professor setting the one across from me straight. "Look," I lectured, "let me tell you something. Ever hear about the Great Famine in Ireland? Around the late 1840s?"

"Hey, is this going to be a two-beer, three-beer, or a what history lesson?"

"I'm giving you the short version. I have to see a man about a dog at eight. So here we go. There was a blight on the potato—the main staple for the Irish."

"Hey, I know all that," he said with a wave of his hand as if he were blowing smoke away. "Get to your point. And don't talk down to me."

"I'm not talking down to you. I'm talking across the table to you."

"I know my history. That's when the Irish came over. And lots of you died on those boats. Like the slaves coming up from Africa. Why are people so mean to each other?"

"Beats me," I shrugged, anxious to get back to the lesson. "My point is that there was food, but the Brits exported it. The Irish call that time the Great Starvation."

"Hey, you're makin' me hungry. How about some chips and salsa? Cut your story real short cuz I've gotta meet a gal about a cat at eight."

"OK. Here's real short. Don't call me Anglo!"

"Your first problem, Gringa, is that you don't know where the hell you are. This isn't Plymouth Rock! This is Nuevo Mexico. We aren't even part of the U.S."

Well, the Chicano and the Irish lass finished the history lesson, along with the beer, the chips and the salsa, and both left around eight to meet the guy, the gal, and the dog and the cat. He got a doctorate in world history and taught in some of the best universities out East. I stayed in his Nuevo Mexico, did the best I could and became a local Anglo. Over the years whenever he visited, the first thing he said when he saw me, even if he had to hang halfway out the window of a pickup and yell across a busy street, was "Hey, Anglo, know where you are yet? C'mon, hop in. I'll buy you a coke over at Rexall's."

The other afternoon, walking over to the post office, I hear someone behind me call out, "Hey, Anglo, I'm back for good. I'm retired!"

I stopped in my tracks, spun around and called back, "Hey, Chicano, your first problem is that you don't know where the hell you are! This isn't the East Coast. No one quits workin' here. C'mon, catch up, and I'll buy you a cup of java down at World Cup."

Funny, how life works, isn't it?

* * *

Thinking that the front desk job would carry me through the summer, I had started reading bulletin boards around town for a place to stay and discovered that the San Geronimo Lodge in Cañon, on the top of Old Witt Road, was renting rooms by the month for $75, no lease, private bath, use of a community kitchen and walking distance to town. I moved in immediately. I could survive here until Labor Day—if I stayed employed—and then return to Santa Cruz to resume an off-season office job at Kennolyn Summer Camp.

Built in 1925, the San G was once a beautiful adobe structure, a resort and dude ranch secluded at the foot of Taos Canyon, surrounded by apricot trees and offering the best of lodging, food and entertainment. The Mamas and the Papas and Bo Diddley played there in the '60s. But now in the late '70s the Grand Old Lady was down on her luck and her heels. The place seemed to be a mix between a hippie commune and an old-fashioned boarding house managed by its owners, Roberta and John Palenchar, transplanted social workers from New York.

Cañoneros called it the Anglo Pueblo. Folks arrived there in VWs, beat up BMWs, Toyotas of every year and model, pickups and motorcycles, by the Greyhound, by their thumb, by a wing and a prayer. They introduced themselves as poets, painters, musicians; as wanderers; as technoshamans and trustafarians; as just passing through; or as lingering '60s hippies wondering whether to stay or leave. Some were trying out Taos and others were trying out themselves; others, like myself, coming from one of the coasts or the Midwest or Puerto Rico or France, were hustling jobs in order to stay in town for the summer and bring this one more dimension into our lives.

Where else could you listen to a free outdoor summer concert of Mozart, Schumann, Rachmaninov and the Americans—Gershwin, Copland and Berlin? A classical pianist used a large corner room at the end of my veranda for his studio. We boarders sat out on the veranda or down on the green grassy grounds beneath his open window listening to him play in the quiet of the rural countryside surrounding the San G. What a pleasure! Several years later I learned that the pianist was composer Noel Farrand, who, along with locals Harold Geller and Richard Cameron-Wolfe had founded Friends for American Music in 1974.

The San G was a bordello for spirits learning the artful difference between earning a living and creating a life. And it was summer. That merciful season that stipples the scars and sorrows of earth and soul with a carousal of color and wantonly splashes the ease of warm, amorous breezes everywhere until all is forgiven, forgotten and everything is a promise once more.

Cañon

This place sprouts sunflowers.
Fields of them! In early blue mornings
I walk through galleries of van Gogh's.

Yellow polka-dotting green alfalfa
fields, splattering black mountains,
dappling brown fences and cows.

I reach town
fully fed
without sweat
of a harvest.

I was told that the best strategy for job hunting was to tell everyone you were looking for work. Everyone! Visit all the art galleries and tell the directors; browse in both bookshops and tell the clerks; have coffee and a sandwich in all the restaurants and beer in all the bars and tell all the waitresses and bartenders. If you wanted a good paying, titled job like the one you had back in your old hometown, leave Taos. Immediately.

DOS

Newspaper Clerk

On my first day of unemployment I went to the newspaper office to buy *The Taos News*, the weekly town paper. Unknowingly, I bumped into a staff worker at the paper and we started to chat.

"I'm off to have coffee and read through the want ads," I told him as I plopped down a quarter on the counter.

"Why? What do you need?"

"A job."

"We've got one."

I started work at the newspaper that afternoon and hated it immediately. After weeks of traveling, a schedule of eight-to-five, five days a week was confining, and after six weeks of fun conversation at a motel front desk, I found answering phones, typing and filing to be tiring mechanical intrusions.

However, working in that newsroom gave me an excellent orientation to Taos. I learned its politics, its local characters, the scandals that got into print or got buried under compassion, where the financial clout was, which issues roused the people and which ones they didn't give a damn about. I also discovered things that weren't listed in the yellow pages—who could patch an adobe fireplace, who had wondrously carved wooden doors from Mexico in his backyard, who had fourth-hand parts for your pickup, and who could teach you how to slaughter your pig.

Town life burst into that newspaper office from the paved streets and dirt roads, from the plaza, the farms, cafés, homes, offices, schools and cantinas of Taos. It came in with the newspaper boys, with the reporters, and with the Taoseños who placed ads, answered ads, bought subscriptions, canceled subscriptions, looked over old issues, handed in letters to the editor, bought advertising space, asked to use our telephone or bathroom or Xerox machine. Only a little of this energy and flow got into print, but all of it got into my grasp of Taos.

Soon I was handling the classified ads. I ran ads selling chickens that laid eggs and chickens that perhaps would lay eggs; old pickups that didn't run so good anymore; firewood, dry or green, in stumps or split, stacked or dumped. I ran ads for stores needing clerks and for clerks needing stores.

Unfortunately, our paper was printed seventy miles away in Santa Fe. My carefully typed and proofed ads were fed to a computer that skipped lines and couldn't spell. Every Wednesday the first paper was sold at the southwest corner of the Taos Plaza at 7:14 a.m. My phone started ringing at 7:15 a.m.

"You didn't put my goddamn phone number in again! How am I gonna sell my wood? I wantcha to run that goddamn ad five more times for free!"

"When ya gonna learn how to spell 'manure'? Where ya from, New York? Who's gonna drive ten miles to get 'menur' even if it is for free?"

"Look, I'm going to start another newspaper in town. This is ridiculous! You haven't gotten one ad right. How am I going to sell land? Who wants 'farty fooded acres with bath and a half. Call for flute lessons before ten p.m.?'"

The scolding voices began to invade my dreams and I could hardly get out of bed on Wednesdays to face the phones. One September afternoon, standing on the office veranda looking north, I saw those tall, slim ethereal aspens, a golden autumn amulet around Taos Mountain, and I asked myself a simple question: What am I doing here?

There was Wheeler Peak to climb, three-hundred-years-old Spanish villages to walk through and Native American pueblos up and down the Río Grande to visit. I needed more time here. I wanted to experience a full year in this town. I was afraid that if I left after summer, it would disappear like Brigadoon and I would never find it again, never find what I would have lost.

Anyway, I figured at $2.50 an hour I ought to at least be happy.

I went inside straight to the editor's office and gave

Billie Blair my two-week notice. "Are you sure?" she asked. "Jobs are hard to find in Taos."

"Yes, Billie, I'm sure."

Then I went out and stood on the veranda again. I stretched under a blue sky so clear I could see right through it, over the low pink adobe roofs of the Plaza straight to the Sangre de Cristos, the southern spur of the Rocky Mountains, flecked with September's reds of the maples and golds of the aspens, where I knew a ski valley was hidden that I had yet to visit.

I hadn't forgotten that it was Taos Pueblo that had lured me to this valley. Often on the weekend, I would park my car at the Kachina Lodge and cross over the cattle guard entering the Pueblo reservation and walk, back in the day when we could, the two miles down Pueblo Road to the village. I'd visit the shops, buy some fry bread or just sit on the low western adobe wall watching the water that came down from Blue Lake flow under the bridge and out to the village.

There I met Manuelita Lujan at one of the ceremonial dances. We just happened to be standing next to each other and had begun to talk. She was short with long dark hair and eyes. She was wearing a beautiful, homemade dress of deerskin leather. She invited me to join her family and friends in a meal at her home. I was honored. Later, on August 4, I drove Manuelita at her request to Santo Domingo Pueblo to celebrate their feast day with her friend Joe García and his family.

I described that day in a poem that I wrote shortly afterward.

Joe García
Santo Domingo/August 4, 1977

Your face …
The dust and heat of the Plaza
bring us to your door.

"Come! Eat!" Your brown arm
sweeps us into your home,
the home of Joe García.
I eat your chile, your posole.
Break bread. Drink your iced tea.

Your wife Sophie and daughter
Rose serve us. I am a stranger
but it is enough that I have
come with Manuelita, your
friend. "Come! Eat!"

Your face …
Your dancing sons and grandsons
come in, painted sweat wrapped
round their chests and arms.
I laugh easily with them and
play with the baby Theresa.

*Driving north at dusk, the open mesas
stretch me out until I remember. Three
weeks ago you had come to the motel
where I work. You were tired
from selling jewelry all day. Many
of your children and Sophie waited
outside in the truck. It was close
to midnight. You were turned away.*

There had been room.

*I remember your face,
Joe García.*

In August, when it seemed that I had in mind to definitely experience the four seasons in New Mexico, I called the Caldwells at Kennolyn Camp in Santa Cruz to tell them of my decision. Marion answered the phone. She was as excited as I was about the adventure that I had embarked on, asked me to send postcards and to call her when I got back. I didn't tell her that I had been fired from my first job and had given a two-week notice to quit my second job.

After Labor Day had come and gone, I was ready to move out of the San G, rent my own little adobe and continue working, making enough money to pay the rent, put gas in my car for weekend sightseeing trips and keep food in the fridge.

On my last day at the newspaper, I took a rental ad over the phone: Large, spacious, one room adobe studio. Vigas. Fireplace. Furnished. Rustic. Secluded Cañon area. $125 a month.

"Before I run this ad, could I see it?"

"Sure. When can you come over?"

"Now."

I walked up the Old Witt Road, turned right, crossed three wooden planks over an irrigation ditch and turned into a yard of aspen, pine and apricot trees. The studio door was open. I walked in.

September's amber light slanted in through windows and a skylight. The cinnamon ceiling vigas were massive, some with a silver patina. Soft white ash lay in the large adobe fireplace possessing one whole corner of the room.

Through the eastern windows I would see daybreak over the Sangre de Cristos. Through the western windows, I would see the pulsing earth forms of mesas, buttes, plateaus and the rim of the western wall of the Río Grande Gorge. I knew I could make a home here until spring.

What I didn't know was the consuming chore of wood gathering for the long, cold Taos winter. I also forgot that I had no winter clothes, having spent the last six years in California. I forgot that my old Toyota

Corolla was disintegrating and I would soon need to trade it in for an equally old but sturdier pickup. But I did not forget that as of the next day, I would be unemployed again.

A "hello" at the open front door spun me around. There stood the landlady, who lived across the yard from the studio. "Geraldine Harvey," she said with outstretched hand. "This was my daughter María's dance studio."

Gerry stood about five-foot one. A robust woman in her fifties. Crow black hair to her waist, a brown cigar in a brown face with smiling brown eyes. She was swathed in a long purple velvet dress with a red waistband. Turquoise and silver bracelets circled both her arms from wrist to elbow.

"I'm Chippewa/Onieda," she said.

"I'm French/Irish." We shook hands again.

Gerry told me that when she and her husband realized the dancing talent of their daughter María, they built the studio for her. María graduated from Taos High and went on to study flamenco in Spain and New York. She was now married and had a son, Paco.

"She's in New York with a flamenco group but she comes back every year to dance in Taos and in Santa Fe. So you'll be able to see her."

I thought if María's strong spirit still inhabited this room then maybe it could strengthen my backbone too. I figured if life brought me to such a wondrous place, it would also bring me the means to sustain it. I moved in the next day.

The summer tourists were gone. The town grew still. Jobs were tight. I was sore from days in the mountains with locals learning how to use a bow saw and axe to gather my winter supply of wood. I struggled in a cold north wind for days cutting plastic to size and stapling it to plywood frames around each window, securing them from winter freezes. I thought of my dad putting up storm windows in Chicago in an hour and a half. When would that invention hit Taos?

GERALDINE AND MARÍA, PLAZA SANTANAIN MADRID, 1962
IN MEMORY
HTTP://HOME.EARTHLINK.NET/~PACANNE/GERALDINEHARVEYALBUM/

The days were growing short and the evening social opportunities, namely one theater and the many scattered bars, made me want to hang my bow saw in a cottonwood and weep for Babylon—warm, easy, scintillating Santa Cruz. Taos was retreating from me, but I was stubborn and wouldn't quit. I had three seasons to go—the rest of fall and then winter and spring.

I would see the elegant María dance at the Taos Community Auditorium when she came back home to visit and I thought of her every time I exercised at her dancing bar along the eastern wall and saw more than I wanted to of myself in the floor-to-ceiling mirror.

Santa Fe Road

For days now
I've wanted to change my name
to Catalina, dye my hair black,
and learn Spanish
fast.

For days now
I've been a torn feather
weighted down by the dust
of these streets, searching
for the warm breast.

For days
I've wanted to run away
until I saw him,
a small brown man,
bent, wearing a sombrero,
walking south on Santa Fe Road.

I stood across the street
and watched him.

I don't know why.

He never looked at me
but as he disappeared
around the corner, he told me

your name is Catherine
your skin is white
your hair light
your language English

and that
is who you are.

The Godfathers – Taos Style

Everyone needs a Godfather. Not the baptismal fount type. More like a Don Corleone.

By October of '77, I had two Godfathers. Don John Holland over at his Rexall Río Grande Drug Store on the Plaza and Don Philip Rael just a few blocks down at the New Mexico Department of Labor. These guys were so powerful they didn't need to break kneecaps. A phone call would do.

After morning coffee at Dori's Bakery and Café and a stop in the main post office, I'd walk two blocks south to the Labor office in Centro Ortiz. With a wave to Stephanie Rivera I'd head over to Mr. Rael's desk. Without looking up he would say, "Is that you again?"

"What do you mean again?"

"Just what I mean. Again." Trying to hide a smile, he'd get on the phone, rasp a word or two and I'd walk out with a handful of interview slips. I never saw Philip standing, but if I did, I would see a tall, handsome man with black hair, dark eyes and always that smile.

Or at lunchtime I'd walk into John's drugstore for a hamburger and fries and he'd greet me with "Do you have a job? Do you have a place to live?" If I said no to either question he'd get on the phone. Who knows what he said over the line but he'd come back with a piece of paper with names and numbers. "Call them," he'd tell me. I'd call them. Problem solved.

As my second job at *The Taos News* was ending, I checked in with Don Rael, the consigliere at the Labor Department.

"Well, I do have something here today, but I don't think it's for you."

"Phil, at least tell me what it is!"

"House cleaning in Talpa."

"Quick, give me the number!"

Within fifteen minutes I drove up to a gracious, sprawling adobe hacienda. The lovely lady of the house, Janet Webb, greeted me with a cup of jasmine tea. We sat before one of her many fireplaces.

"Catherine, I'll be glad to show you around and tell you what I'm looking for, but I don't think this is for you."

Were my fingernails too clean? Was there a seal on my forehead visible only to her of my master's degree in English? Was she clairvoyant and knew that I had held jobs with titles like "director" and "head?"

I cleared my throat. My voice got down on its knees.

"Please, Janet, let me clean your house."

TRES

The Housekeeper

I had found the best job in Taos. I set my own days and hours. Flexibility was top priority. If there were a dance at a pueblo or a chance to go to Santa Fe, it was an easy matter to switch a day. Does it really matter when a house is dusted?

It was a two-hundred-year-old hacienda. Through the years when a son or daughter married and brought their spouse home, a room was added. The home grew as the family grew.

Two Spanish ladies came once a week to do the constant patching that adobes need. These are organic homes, arising out of the earth and weathering like the earth. The women moved through the house with their buckets of fresh adobe made from backyard dirt, water and straw that they had mixed themselves for patching walls, fireplaces and steps. They also carried a big pail of calcimine and water for whitewashing. They kept an eye on the ceiling for leaks because between the vigas and the herringbone pattern of narrow aspens was a foot of dirt. When they finished the last room and it was new again, they started all over.

I patched up the weathering of the Bell family. Larry,

an internationally known sculptor with a studio in Taos, collected guitars and played them, collected hats and wore them, collected friends and loved them. I got to dust the guitars and hats and meet the friends. Zara, a spirited three-year-old whose play area was the whole house, helped me make the beds, wash the dishes and take the ashes from the fireplaces that had been used during the night. And when she went to nursery school or off to take a nap, I did everything all over again.

Janet, a fashion illustrator who still maintained a studio in New York, was concentrating on renovating her home; raising and slaughtering pigs, goats, sheep and turkeys; organic gardening; teaching an art course in town; and caring for her family and the guests in every bedroom.

It was an exciting family. I had morning coffee with them, shared the small and big happenings of our Taos lives, cleaned their toilet bowls and attended their cocktail parties.

For the first month, I couldn't lift my right arm to brush my hair or bend over without straightening up slowly with a groan. During the night, I woke up with every turn and wondered what rare terminal disease I had.

But as the year peeled itself bare, the soreness dissolved. I would see spring! Of course, that depended on how transparent the Taos mud would be.

No corporate employee ever received the fringe

benefits I did. Jars of Janet's exquisite canning: apricot butter with orange, India relish, lemon rosemary jelly and new growths from her one hundred houseplants.

"Do any of these slacks fit you?"

"Do you need a warming pan?"

"Could you use this light fixture?"

I felt good about this work. There was no desire to come late or leave early or to take long coffee breaks. No one needed to draw me a flow chart in five colors of the hierarchical structure of the system. It was just Janet, me, and my pink rubber gloves.

Through all the cleaning, dusting and mopping, my mind was free. Free to meditate on a dance I had seen the day before at a Native American pueblo or consider a conversation I had that morning over coffee at Foster's Café on East Kit Carson Road with a couple of Taoseños, to nurture the beginnings of a poem or reflect upon how my life was unfolding.

The willingness to clean toilet bowls is liberating. Wherever in the world there are such bowls, one can find work. Sort of like fulfilling the prophecy "the lowly shall be mighty"—in their way. I draw the line, however, at outhouses and open pits.

But at $37.50 a week, I needed another part-time job.

QUATRO

The Caregiver

Many a late afternoon I sat at my landlady's kitchen table with one or more Cañoneros enjoying a drink and conversation. What I loved most was hearing their stories of Taos and of its sons and daughters. Colorful, outrageous, unbelievable—but no doubt all true.

One afternoon when it was just Gerry and myself, the conversation turned to my need of another part-time job. Immediately we were in her car, off to see her friend Virginia Starquist, who needed someone on the weekends to care for her elderly mother and an invalid friend. Since I loved stories, caring for a woman who was reliving her 1890s New England childhood and another who was wandering through WWI as a war nurse again was perfect.

Virginia had one of the few good-paying jobs in Taos: a geologist at the Molycorp Mine in Questa. She had come to Taos some twenty years ago and over the years had built a large, comfortable house on Blueberry Hill. Two years earlier, she had brought her elderly mother out from Vermont. Her mother was the Yankee woman I had met in American Lit. 101: devoted to her New England farm, healthy, well educated, finely mannered, a delightful conversationalist with that notorious dry Yankee wit and a huge memory bank of aphorisms.

But lately the past had more of a gravitational pull on her than the present. In her nineties, now living among sagebrush and piñon, she wanted to hitch up the horses and head on home. Ma and Pa were waiting.

Virginia was also caring for Miss Adams, her college teacher, mentor and friend, whom she had moved from New England to Taos. Miss Adams was up in years and now an invalid. She was born of aristocracy in a century now vanished. She could not remember her mother ever coming to dinner in anything but a formal gown.

The young Evelyn Adams was also brilliant, beautiful and independent. She set out immediately to get the maximum use from her wealth and class. Educated here and abroad, she became proficient in languages, math and physics, and received a degree in architecture.

She asked her father if she could join the army in World War I. "You can do whatever you want," he told her, "but do it well." With that, he gave Evelyn an overcoat and a revolver. For the duration of the war, she directed a hospital in France.

Back in New York, she became the first female licensed auto mechanic. Then on to long years of involvement with archaeological excavations in Greece, drawing the floor plans of the sites to scale. She prowled around Africa and Asia Minor. "I always had my own little trench going someplace," she told Virginia. She was an CIA agent after World War II. "When Warsaw fell, I had to do something."

She then went on to turn a hobby into a profession and became curator of the Yale coin collection at the Sterling Library, retiring at seventy-five and writing her last published monograph at eighty.

Now in her late eighties, too frail to walk or talk, she needed someone to help her through these last relentless days. The morning bath. Dress her. Feed her breakfast. Settle her in the living room. Wash her clothes and bed linens. Feed her lunch. Again and again.

"Catherine, you may find this work unattractive. Sometimes Miss Adams gets into a bad mood and there's biting and screaming. Of course, she's not striking out at you. It's her life, the way it was and the way it is now. What do you think? Want to try it?"

Although I answered immediately, a series of flashbacks brought into focus some hard days of my past.

Sister Pauline. Energy streaming from her. Hearing her laughter first, seeing her bright eyes second. A teacher and published poet. As a young nun (a story for another day), I looked up to her as someone who was fully alive.

Then she came home to our motherhouse in La Grange, Illinois, just outside of Chicago. To die of cancer. In the room next to mine. In those nights, when she would moan and I would wake, I broke the Grand Silence and I broke the rule that an unprofessed sister should not speak to a professed one. Night after night, I went into her room, sat at the edge of her bed, picked her up and rocked her in my lap. I was terrified, had never seen so minutely the hourly coming of death. Where does the brightness of eyes go? The redness of cheeks? The soft roundness of a body?

My father. I came home from California with my sleeping bag during a cold Chicago winter so I could lie on the floor next to Dad's hospital bed during the nights. At two in the morning we played gin rummy, at three I wheeled him through the corridors, at four I rubbed his back, at five he slept, at six the doctors woke him up to ask him how he was. I was waiting for the day Dad would say, "Why, doctors, don't you know I'm dying?"

We wanted Dad home so we learned how to give pain shots for the cancer every four hours. My sister Mary was a nurse and she lined the family up at the kitchen counter with alcohol, cotton, a hypodermic needle and an orange. We practiced, dreading our first turn.

I remember mine. It was past midnight. Still another thirty minutes or so to go for a shot, but Dad's light was on. He was sitting on the edge of the bed, his head hanging down between two sharp ridges of shoulder blade—so much flesh gone. I thought the hell with the schedule. He needs that shot now. I took the tray from the kitchen counter and joked as I knelt before him. He rolled his pajama leg up to mid-thigh. I knew to avoid hard spots or black and blue spots. I searched for a soft place, rubbed it with a pad of cotton soaked in alcohol, pinched a pocket of skin together, then flattened it and inserted the hypodermic needle as deftly as I could, but it stuck and came out raggedly. I saw blood. I was sick. I wanted to run away from the sorrow and terror of this death. I looked up.

"I'm sorry, Dad."

"Huh? You mean you're done? Best nurse I've ever had!"

Of course, what he meant was, "Look, this is hard for all of us and it's no one's fault. So let's just do it with as much good humor as we can. And thanks for being with me." Dad died three years later, February of 1974.

Now it was Virginia before me who needed help with her mom and her good friend.

"Yes, Virginia, I'd like to try."

I tried. I tried very hard. Virginia was lovely. My caring for her mother and Miss Adams freed her on the weekends for a day in Santa Fe or lunch in Taos with friends or work in her study or in her garden or doing what she loved most—cooking.

Every Saturday and Sunday I was called to join Virginia and her mother for lunch. Roast duckling, meat loaf, Spanish rice, rum cake, Key Lime pie. She cooked from one of her fifty-seven cookbooks or from memory or inspiration.

I will always remember those lunches. Virginia talked of her life. A childhood in New England. A commitment to a profession. Her travels in this country and abroad. But what I loved most were her stories of Taos in the '50s and '60s. Stories of the town, of its people and their ways.

Miss Adams and I had our own routine. She loved her morning highball and the promise of it got us through her bath and dressing. I got to know her eating habits, how to prepare her food and coax her to eat. I held her hands, stroked her face and carried on long monologues with her. Her eyes told me she was glad to still be participating in family life.

But I forgot to distance myself emotionally from the age and poignant senility of Virginia's mom and the helplessness and dependency of Miss Adams. I began to wonder about myself. How would my journey end? Would I be able to care for myself? What was I doing now to prepare for that? Neither job paid any benefits and both could end tomorrow without notice, without unemployment insurance. As the days went on, I became depressed thinking about my lack of money, of things, of the impracticality of my lifestyle.

One morning, the bathing and dressing of Evelyn was particularly difficult. She was weak and uncooperative. By the time I got her to her chair in the living room, I was exhausted. I needed a drink, too. Mrs. Starquist came up to us in tears, sobbing that her daughter Virginia had gone off to Vermont that morning without her. She didn't know what she had done to be treated so badly, to be left alone in a strange house.

I took her into my arms, pressed my cheek against hers. That at ninety, one should come to this! I tried to sooth her with words she did not understand. Over her shoulder, I saw Miss Adams crumpled in her chair like a puppet with cut strings, looking up at me pleading, "Drink. Drink."

At that moment I experienced what James Joyce called an epiphany. Those rare, spontaneous moments when one transcends bones and names and needs and feels with one's gut a truth so clearly that there is no doubting it, no forgetting it. Fiery as a burning bush or silent as under the Bodhi Tree or mysterious as awakening from a dream, I knew at that moment that ultimately all we have is one another.

And I knew I had to leave this job. But how? I had grown close to these three ladies. Who would Virginia get to replace me? How would I explain my feelings to her, she who lived twenty-four hours a day in this situation? Would the next person really care about these dear old ladies?

Miss Adams graciously died in her sleep that night.

I received the call early Sunday morning. It was a day of liberation for both Miss Adams and me. Virginia told me that she would be able to care for her mom. "Mom really doesn't need a lot of care. It was Evelyn that I didn't have the physical energy for. Thanks so much for your time here, Catherine. You were a great help."

* * *

All of a sudden the gift of a whole day lay outside my window, beneath the apricot and aspen trees thin in December, in the forest trails hidden up in the mountains, on the Old Witt Road that followed the Río de Don Fernando de Taos down to town.

I chose town. The two-mile walk along the river, as it wended its way to town, was one of my favorites. In the spring, every farmer and gardener cleaned out their irrigation ditch and diverted their allotted water from a nearby acequia to water their land. The whole of the first mile I looked straight ahead, mesmerized by the mesa west of the Río Grande Gorge leading to Arizona. That pale blue breadth of sky, the dark green strip of sagebrush, those deep arroyos and buttes, that slice of cold white snow were all vibrating under the huge New Mexican sky. In Chicago it was the lakefront, in California the ocean, here it was the mesa across the Gorge that lifted me above the daily pattern.

Troubles fell away as I walked the land. Each adobe, each wooden barn, each outhouse, shack, shed, fence was unique. It reflected the owner's needs, skills, the weariness of one day, and the exuberance of another.

There were more fences than anything else. Low adobe walls, stone walls, wood posts several yards apart strung with wire or laced with wood planks. They fenced in cows, horses, sheep, goats, chickens and pigs; alfalfa, corn and bean fields; yards of kids and laundry;

and, of course, cars with the hoods up and tires off, iceboxes, sofas without cushions, and cabinets without drawers—all with parts that someday might be useful.

My first stop was Dori's Bakery. It was next to the post office, so picking up your mail and stopping in Dori's seemed to go together. You'd stomp the December snow off or scrape the mud from your feet and step into the smells of a busy bakery, the warmth of ovens and bodies and a fireplace, the sound of music and talk and dishes.

I shared a tiny round table with Tom, a fellow who once had done a stint as an aerospace engineer in Southern California and now repaired wind instruments. He hadn't missed an AA meeting in the two years he'd been here. He knew all about losing jobs.

"How's life?" he asked.

"I lost one of my part-time jobs."

"It's not the worst thing that can happen, is it?" he asked.

"Nope."

"And you know, the more you cut back, the less you need to break your back for dough."

"Yeah, I guess it's time to read Walden again. Simplify. Simplify."

"And this is the place you can do it."

"Can do it? You have to do it!"

"You can learn to carry your own weight. Take care of yourself a little more and not call the goddamn repairman all the time. Or keep running into the stores.

Hell, some of these Chicanos born and raised here shame me. They can practice law or run a shop or teach school but they can still go up to the mountains and hunt and fish, cut down trees to burn in their fireplaces. They tune up their own trucks, add a room to their home—plumbing, electricity, the whole bit."

"And you should taste their chile!" Dori had joined us. "Catherine, come work for me. I need someone about twenty hours a week. Minimum wage. $2.30 an hour. It's fun. And you know everyone already. Think about it. I've got to go pull a pie out."

"See," Tom said, "it's easier here, especially with friends."

The bakery would be hard. It's one thing to walk in at ten a.m. and have coffee and a bagel with cream cheese with friends, and another experience to struggle in at seven a.m. and bake, wash dishes, wait tables, sweep up, handle the cash register and walk away tired and sweaty, with $2.30 an hour less taxes in your hand. But I didn't have a choice. I needed work.

I walked through town on the way back to stop at an art gallery. When I had worked at the newspaper, the gallery owner had called and offered me a job. Then I wasn't interested. But now I needed work.

The small gallery was well off the beaten path. The owner was in. I didn't know how he got his fantasy that I had a background in fine arts, was a super saleswoman, and committed to the Taos art scene, but I wouldn't divest him of it—not yet.

"I'd love to have you in the gallery! What time is good for you?"

"Oh, maybe around three days a week. Five hours each day is all I need."

"Fine! Do you want to work on commission?"

Ever since Labor Day I was loving Taos more because the tourists were gone and it was just we locals. But we didn't buy art!

"No, I'd feel safer with a straight $3.00 an hour."

"Fine! When can you start?"

"I'll get in touch with you in a day or so."

I walked back up the Old Witt Road. This time it was the mountains straight ahead. I felt as expansive as they looked. I had lost a job that morning and by noon had been offered two. I had arrived! Taos knew I was here. At least this morning.

By the time I passed the first cow, her four feet planted in thistles, her mouth twisting around a six-foot sunflower stalk, I had made my decision.

CINCO

The Art Gallery Sitter

It was the wrong decision. I discovered immediately why the job is called "sitting" a gallery. Sitting a morgue with an occasional relative or police officer coming in to identify a body would have been livelier. I truly "sat" the gallery.

No one came in except the UPS. The local Anglos only visited the galleries for openings, at least those where wine and finger-food were served. The Hispanics seldom came. "What business are they of mine?" they asked me. The summer tourists, of course, crowded the galleries, many with serious intent to buy. But this was winter, deep in December, and the skiers came to ski.

I spent those quiet, sparkling winter afternoons sitting by the fireplace reading. I recalled the threatening slate skies of cold Chicago winters of my childhood. By five p.m. both the school day and the late afternoon hours of play were over. It was nearing suppertime when it was good to be safe and warm inside.

My favorite refuge in those days, when I beat my sister Mary there, was the long living room radiator hidden behind the sofa, under the front windows of our brick bungalow. The radiator had a cover on it and I would lie on my stomach stretched out, hidden from my brother and sisters. There in the darkening living room lit by the soft yellow streetlight I could peer through the slats of the Venetian blinds and see our neighbors, bundled and bent, homeward bound on the icy sidewalks. Ours, though, was always neatly shoveled by Dad or us kids. In summer, when I wasn't playing outside, that's where I read all my Nancy Drew mysteries .

Mother was young and busy with her family. The kitchen's bright light and noises were muffled by the time they reached the living room. Mother called, "Pat, it's your turn to set the table!" The icebox opened and closed, the frying pan lid came down and the pork chops simmered until Dad came home. The timer went off. The boiling potatoes were turned low; their pot's bouncing lid quieted. Each fork, each knife, each plate was set down on the table. Six sets. The faucet turned on to fill Dad's water glass. Mother called Chuck to wash his hands. Chuck was in his own childhood world of the back porch, making a model airplane, listening to *Captain Midnight*. Then Mother came into the living room and in the dark—perhaps not knowing that beyond the sofa I was lying on the radiator—sat and played the piano until Dad came home. I heard the click of her wedding ring on the keys. *Stella by Starlight. Our Love Affair. Nola.* How safe I was then. Supper almost ready and Dad on his way home.

Those reveries were always interrupted by the gallery owner pulling up a chair between me and the warmth of the fire and expounding to his captive audience on his grand vision for Taos.

"We're planning a really fine art auction this spring. We want to bring the right kind of people to Taos and use the money raised to build a school of dance or maybe opera or … ." On and on the dreamer went. "This town needs culture."

"Needs culture?" I challenged him. "Over a thousand years of Native American civilization, close to four-hundred years of Spanish and Mexican life, and now La Raza. The Buffalo Dance, the Deer Dance, the drums, polkas, fandangos, flamenco, guitar, fiestas, santos, tin and iron work, the weaving at Chimayó …." I was on a roll. A furious one.

"Oh, that," the owner cut in. He yawned, got up and left the gallery.

Usually, whenever the owner left, Jeff popped in. He was also a painter, with blue eyes and a mop of white hair, whose small studio was close by. He'd sit down and warm himself by our fire. Now I was his captive audience and he would let go a few salvos at the owner and "his kind."

"They come and go. I've seen more dang people try out more dang ideas here. Taos Mountain just eats them up and spits them out. You'll see."

On Christmas Eve I asked the owner if he were going to the Pueblo for Vespers and the bonfires. It was going to be my first Christmas Eve in Taos and I was excited.

"I never go to the Pueblo. It's too commercial."

"Too commercial? A living museum and they ask for a buck to save up for a new J.C. Penny blanket while you and your art and dance buddies are selling Taos right under our noses to New Yorkers and Texans!"

The owner left. Three minutes later Jeff popped in.

"Look at all this crap hanging up. See that mesa landscape over there? When that's sold, that old painter's going to slap another just like it on another canvas only bigger. And the more wall space the owner gets, the more crap he's going to hang up and the more money in his pocket. I tell you one of these days that old Mountain's going to kick the hell out of these bloodsuckers.

"Why, I just gave a painting away. Young kid from Ann Arbor really wanted one but didn't have any money. I said, 'Look, you want it? It's yours. Send me some money when you can.' Damn, a thing belongs to those who want it most."

I cobbled these two jobs together and they advanced me like a counter across the game of chance I was playing: to survive one year in Taos. But both jobs ended abruptly.

The owner and I had one more fireside chat a few days later.

"I met a marvelous woman working at another gallery. She lives, breathes and eats art."

"Oh."

"She's a painter, too. A good one."

"Oh."

"But she'll come only if she can work full time."

"Are you trying to tell me this is my last day here?"

"Well, sort of."

I walked out onto the cold, snowy December streets of Taos and looked at the Mountain, blue black, its head inaccessible in billowing gray snow clouds.

"Hey, you," I said to it, "I've just been fired. Sort of. Are you giving me a message? Sort of?"

It wasn't long before I heard word that the gallery owner had packed his bags in a huff and left town.

Nevertheless, Winter Solstice arrived, turning us all toward the light. Winter feasts of the religious liturgical year, the pre-Christian festivals underlying them, and the great ceremonies of Taos Pueblo converged to illuminate our cosmic story.

At the Pueblo, I watched the young ones absorb the rituals of their elders. I watched them grow quiet, their eyes big, their bodies still as stone. The smell of incense scented their hair; the drumbeats reverberated in their growing bones. Smoke from the bonfires clung to their jackets; dance and excitement swirled around them. Sprigs of evergreen lay fallen before their feet. In my imagination I could almost hear them say *This is who we are. This is where we're from. This is what we do.*

Those of us who had come late to this land were transfixed and something took hold of us. Something unshakable.

1978

It Continues

> *"We're all just walking one another home."*
> — RAM DASS

Keeping On, Keeping On

The New Year of 1978 found me back at $37.50 a week. I was weary of hustling part-time jobs, of cobbling them into a full-time job, of learning the new names and the new ropes. I felt beaten.

Since my plan was only to stay a year, I didn't want to go for better jobs which would require time and energy to train me with expectations of future contributions from me. Besides, after having taught for eleven years with a master's degree, I had a high expectation of the kind of work I could love and grow in.

Nevertheless, I humbly confessed to the Godfathers that I had lost four jobs in seven months and was in need of yet another one. I did take credit for hanging on to my housekeeping job. Secure in the knowledge that the Godfathers would be working the phones on my behalf, I got into my green forest service pick-up that I had purchased from Silva's Auto in Colorado and spent the day driving through the high country, stopping at each village to walk its roads, visit its churches, stop at its cafés or tiendacitas for a bite to eat and chat with the locals.

During these long winter days, the dark side of the year, I was absorbing into my bones and spirit the physical and social isolation of these northern New Mexico villages. A people abandoned by Spain, by Mexico, by the United States. A people in a mountainous, arid, rugged terrain left to their own resources, their own wit, their own determination. Aliens outside their land and now—through chicanery, ignorance, coercion resulting in the loss of lands, of old life styles, of their colonial economic system—they were becoming estranged from this place that they had inhabited since the 1500s.

I saw the beautifully handcrafted Spanish church at Las Trampas standing since 1750, still used by the Penitentes during Holy Week. I saw adobe farm houses dissolving back to the earth they had come from, like we, too, will do some day. It was a countryside crisscrossed by deeply rutted dirt roads, flocks of grazing sheep, smoke from every flat adobe roof top. I visited small fenced camposantos—cemeteries falling down a hillside, straining up another—and the weaving looms of Chimayó, hundreds of years old.

How many of these fathers and grandfathers had to leave their poor farm to work the beet and potato fields of Colorado or herd sheep in Montana, sometimes coming back no better off than when they had left? How many of these women knew of no other reality than the relentless day-to-day duel with life, of improvising, of making do, of going without?

And there I was, living among them. Instead of struggling with the gods through land and rainfall and livestock, I struggled as an "outsider" through the vagaries of low-paying jobs, the lack of a foothold or political pull or family connections.

I saw money flowing in and out of town, the lights at night getting bigger and brighter, land being bought up. I sensed change and a heady time a-coming.

I also saw the red sky at morning, its reflection spread over the western mesa in alternating stripes of pastel pinks and purples, waiting for the day to come for one more go at life. I walked for hours in the canyons and up on the hillsides. I wore old clothes, burned wood, read and wrote. I had time to stop and stare and to know and need my neighbor. Imperceptibly, I was being assimilated into a culture that had been formed by the mating of a people and a land.

I think of my great-grandparents, the La Plants, the Furlongs, the Naylors coming from French Canada, Ireland and England, stepping like me so unprepared into a strange place.

Northern New Mexico is a mirror. It reflects one's strengths and weaknesses, one's values and needs, the degree of one's ingenuity and resilience.

After my walks, it was always good to return to María's studio, a squat, thick-walled, flat-roofed fortress, now outlined in snow but in summer surrounded by six-feet tall red hollyhocks.

But still the ever nagging, "What am I doing here?"

Then I remembered Gypsy Boy, a pastel painting by my dad's mom, Katherine Leahy Naylor, my namesake. She gave it to my parents as a wedding present. It was a portrait of a young boy's head and shoulders. His thick, tousled black curls fell beneath a floppy, brown felt hat. A blue and green peacock feather stuck in the hat's rim gave him a festive look. His skin was a warm brown, his hooded eyes, lashes, and eyebrows were coal black, his lips a delicate red. Shoulders emerged from a sleeveless brocade vest, a textured material of muted golds and russets, buttoned at the neck. He was sweet. Pensive. Full of the future. Although he faced the viewer, his eyes looked off to the right.

There was absolutely no one like him in my family. He was everything kept under lock and key, everything held in secret, and everything that I wanted to know and experience. He was a part of me that would lie so deeply hidden, so profoundly unknown, for so long.

Mom said that as soon as I learned how to push a chair next to the dining room buffet, I'd climb up and talk to him, getting my finger prints all over the painting's glass. We called him Gypsy Boy. He was my first love.

"GYPSY BOY" BY MY DAD'S MOM, KATHERINE LEAHY NAYLOR

Mom always described me as "different." "The Gypsies left her at my doorstep," she would say with a raised eyebrow. Because her smile and tone of voice held both pride and admonition, I didn't know whether to be proud or embarrassed. She had other code expressions for the same sentiment. "You're just like your Uncle John." Uncle John, Dad's older brother, said he always had to see what was on the other side of a mountain until the Pacific Ocean stopped him.

When I was around ten years old, I use to come home from grammar school, turn on the television and lie on the living room floor in front of the console, with its doors closed and the volume turned down. I only wanted to see the little red light at the bottom of the console. Then I would stare at its unwavering brightness and begin hypnotizing myself, imagining whatever country my grade was studying, and ask the same questions over and over: If I were born in Japan (or Egypt, or Sweden …), who would I be? What would I look like? What would I wear? What language would I speak? What would my family be like? My mother? My father? I didn't know then that I was wondering how much of me wasn't me, but rather artifacts of the culture into which I had been born.

If I asked my mother any of these questions, she would say, "Cathy, you think too much. You're going to wear out your brain."

I came to know that being a dreamer, living in an imaginary world with imaginary playmates, wandering, getting lost, and asking unusual questions made one different. I was always seeking that other, larger world—the world where Gypsy Boy lived.

Eventually I stopped talking about my imaginary escapades and they disappeared, lying in wait deep in my unconscious, and I entered full heartedly into happy years of growing up like everyone else.

SEIS

Front Desk Clerk – Again!

"Catherine, it's Phil from the unemployment office. I've been trying to get you all day."

"Oh, I've been out. Driving around your country. It's so beautiful. So strong and peaceful."

"I know. That's why I came back from Salt Lake City. My wife and I were making more than a thousand a month, but we missed Taos. We wanted our kids to grow up here."

"Yeah, I think I'd miss it too. Maybe I'm stuck here now."

"Look, are you out of work as usual?"

"As usual! What do you mean? I've been working my ass off in this town."

"I know. I know. Just kidding. I've got a job for you. I wasn't going tell anyone 'til I talked with you."

"What is it?"

"Front desk clerk. Part-time."

"Where?"

"Can't tell you over the phone. You have to come in and fill out the interview form."

"Phil, I'm not coming all the way into town just to find out which motel it is. And you know I wouldn't go on an interview without your form."

"Indian Hills."

"Forget it!"

"Didn't you work there once?"

"Exactly. Forget it!"

"Well, there's one more."

"Which one?"

"The Inn."

I wanted to say forget it again. A national chain of hotels. A sterile, expensively mimeographed building sitting on the outskirts of town, ablaze with lights. There was nothing adobe about it. No cottonwoods shaded it. No colorful hollyhocks softened it. A parasite blighting the Northern New Mexico rural countryside, hiring the town people at minimum wage while charging its guests top rates. My hands may not sweat, but my heart would. This would be survival, though, at least through spring.

"Okay, Phil. I'll come in for the interview slip tomorrow. Thanks for the call."

Having had previous front desk experience in Taos and being the first to interview, I was hired immediately. I was offered two mornings and three evenings at minimum wage. I rearranged my housekeeping job that had been reduced to one day a week because the Bells were tightening their financial belt. If I squeezed mine anymore, I'd squeeze the breath out of me.

The manager, who missed his true calling of drill sergeant, saw me as fodder for his platoon's front line. All the military rigmarole was there: the uniforms, the nametags, the time clock, the policies and procedures, the bulletin board to be checked daily, the threatening memos. I must have been out of town when the military coup took place.

Every day was the same at the front desk: punch the clock; clip on your name tag; smile; count your opening cash; book in people; post telephone, bar and restaurant charges as they came across the desk; look busy whenever Sarge walked by; answer the telephone; make reservations; and deal with the endless questions of guests.

"How much snowfall have you had in the last thirty hours?"

"Is it going to snow tonight?"

"What kind of snow is up at the Ski Valley? Wet? Soft? Hard packed?"

I lived without radio or TV. If it were cold, I'd put on another sweater. If it rained on my laundry, I'd leave it out for another day to dry. If it looked cloudy at night with a large, soft yellow halo around the moon, I'd bring in another stack of wood should I wake to a snowy morning. If I stepped out my door onto good staying snow and had the time, I'd put my cross country skiing gear into my truck, pack some good lunch food and head up to U.S. Hill. That's how I lived.

So I suggested to these blue nylon, down-padded, jump-suited ski buffs that they call the state police or buy the morning paper or listen to the next news broadcast on their radio or TV or go into the lounge and ask another guest who's been here a few days and was recording the weather hourly in a pocket notebook.

They walked away, looking over their shoulder. No radio? No TV? Doesn't know the exact snow score? Unbelievable.

If I'm hired at minimum wage, I figure that's my boss's way of saying, "Look, this job isn't that important. Anyone can do it. There's no great responsibility."

But, in reality, if at the end of a desk clerk's shift the paper work and cash count didn't balance, the clerk stayed until it did. Many a time I came to find the preceding front desk clerk still there. Drawn, weary, angry. Register tapes, room folios, record sheets, tallies, forms strewn all over the front desk.

Too bad about children to be picked up or a second job to go to or a candlelight supper planned weeks in advance. And if the clerk never balanced the cash count, the shortage came out of their pocket. Could the manager have miscounted when he made change? Did an error go unchecked from the previous shift? Was the error in the paper work and not the register drawer?

"Tough," the Inn said. "Pay up."

My co-workers humanized boot camp with their

humor and unflagging spirits. I enjoyed many a coffee break with Orlando who chose to come to the United States rather than be taken a political prisoner in his native Argentina. His American wife Joan, a ski instructor, chose Taos. From university professor to restaurant host, from a sophisticated South American city to a northern New Mexico town, Orlando shared his journey with me. It was a hard one.

I took my supper breaks with the waitresses, all from Taos, who talked of marrying their high school sweethearts; their kids; their one trip to California; their cherished grandmothers still living by themselves in their nineties, carrying their own water, using outhouses and refusing every modern convenience from their children except television.

Joe Medina, the marvelous chef, explained the intricacies of the ancient system of irrigation to me, gave me gardening tips and slipped me the first of his supper sopaipillas. I remember Her Serene Highness Rogeria Meecham, who served Medina's great food. I remember Marcella Cárdenas, José Valencia, Tanya Montoya, Fabi Arellano. I remember dear Ben Quintana carrying room service trays by the front desk and sneaking me a dessert. I remember Pearl Trujillo, Nancy Madrid, Josie Vargas, Pat Mondragón and Jean Gaitlan. I remember the locals stopping by the front desk to schmooze on their way to the lounge. And Sarge, with security cameras for eyes, watching it all.

But most of all I remember Joe Ray Romero, my front desk partner. During our long evenings he told me stories of growing up in Taos. He still lived with his parents and five of his eleven brothers and sisters. He told me of being punished in grammar school for speaking Spanish. "Hell, I never even heard English until first grade." He told me of summer days as a kid horseback riding to the hot springs, spending the whole day picnicking. Of the endless cutting, hauling and splitting of wood with his dad and older brothers. Of his army years and everything he had seen and of his lonesomeness for Taos.

"My compadres are here! My people! I drive down the streets and honk at everyone. This is my home." He couldn't understand why we Anglos left our homes to come to his home, although I kept reminding him that I was just visiting.

Since the Inn had a coffee shop, a dining room, a conference room and a lounge with evening music, many of the townspeople came in. It was a great opportunity for me to see old friends, be introduced to new ones, and catch the town news. In the evenings, the lounge drew the night people. Joe Ray knew them all. After a rapid-fire exchange of greetings in Spanish, they shifted to English to include me. Some remembered me from The Indian Hills.

"I never met anyone who can get jobs in Taos like you. But why the hell can't you keep them?"

"Long story," I'd reply.

One glorious Sunday in February I went cross-country skiing deep into the solitary winter beauty of the Sangre de Cristos. Hours later I returned to my truck ahead of my friends and spent the time talking with another skier, who happened to be a Taos Municipal School Board member.

"So you're a teacher! Why didn't you sign up with us last fall?"

"I assumed you were over-supplied with teachers like California, where I came from. Plus, I don't really know how long I'll be here."

"Look, we're really hurting for good substitute teachers. From this point on it's ski accidents, the flu, what have you. So as long as you're here, we sure can use you. Get into the superintendent's office tomorrow and get your papers in order. The school Board meets on the fourteenth. I'll see that you get in."

I couldn't believe it. After eight years of being out of the classroom, Taos, this tough-ass town, was giving me the chance California never did. I got my papers in, and on Valentine's Day of 1978 the Board approved me as a K-twelve substitute teacher. I was thrilled. After going through six jobs in my first nine months in Taos, I finally had a foot in my profession.

I informed Sarge that I needed to give up my two mornings, but would keep my three nights and be available weekends. A good deal for him, I thought.

"Absolutely not," he barked. "To be of use to us you have to be available twenty-four hours a day, seven days a week." His mouth clamped down on the imaginary pin of a hand grenade. His eyes turned to bullets. I had been dishonorably discharged. Case closed.

The next day a new schedule of hours was posted on the bulletin board. My name was not on the list. I lasted a month and a half. I went into the lounge, dropped a quarter in the jukebox on Johnny Paycheck's "Take This Job and Shove It" and walked out to make the farewell rounds. Joe Ray was alone at the front desk.

"Hey, buddy," I said laying down a couple of dollars, "let me have some quarters." I stacked up the quarters and pushed them over to him. "Do me a favor. Keep that song playing. It will drive Sarge nuts."

> *Take this job and shove it*
> *I ain't workin' here no more.*
> *Ya better not try and stand in my way*
> *Cause I'm walkin' out the door.*
> *Take this job and shove it*
> *I ain't workin' here no more.*

I got in my truck and drove away. I was now making a cool fifteen bucks a week for one day of housework. Substitute teaching sounded like a precarious proposition.

SIETE

Substitute Teacher

The next morning I got up early, put on a pot of coffee, turned on KKIT for morning news, dressed for school and sat at the kitchen table waiting for the phone to ring. Waiting for Job Number 7 to show its face.

That first week my phone does not ring. Not once.

On Saturday I'm faced with a repair bill for my truck. My one day of housekeeping would pay for half of it.

By Sunday I knew it was time to go to the Taos Pueblo. Time to visit one of my sacred places. Time to get perspective on the art of survival.

I parked my truck at the main post office, had a quick cup of coffee at Dori's and, once again, headed out on foot to the Pueblo through the back dirt roads. I walked northeast through the flat sagebrush. Over my left shoulder, to the west, the flat mesa stretched out endlessly, a loophole for the spirit when it needs to soar. In front of me, to the northeast, curved the Sangre de Cristo Mountains, holding in their embrace since the tenth century the roots and genius of a people. They are called the Blood of Christ because in winter the setting western sun sets aflame their snowy peaks.

After ten minutes of walking, the landscape changes.

Piñon trees and chokeberry bushes brought the land up to me. I walked past fields not yet turned over for spring planting. Past grazing cows and horses. Fences defined the road and I began wondering how many feet have traversed this same road over the centuries. Across the Río Grande, up from Mexico, down from the mountains, across the Plains. How many ideas and causes, how many hopes and schemes, petitions and plunder have these feet brought?

And now I come. A pilgrim on foot. To one of the great marketplaces of the world. To seek what it knows.

Then, suddenly, through the bare January treetops, I see it. The tan top of the South Pueblo. I stop, letting my life encounter the spirit of this place springing up anew each day from a dialogue started over a thousand years ago between a people and the land wherein they dwell.

I enter the great Plaza through a break in a low adobe wall. The Río Pueblo, coming down from Blue Lake high in the Native American's sacred Taos Mountain, splits the Plaza in half. The North Pueblo, its massive brown walls rising up, each level retreating in natural rhythms, floor by floor; and mirroring it across the Plaza, is the South Pueblo. Five levels of wood hewn ladders. The windows are tiny but perfectly square. Simple wood doors painted the colors of the rainbow. The Pueblo looks unreal, diminutive, a ghost village but as I approach, I see smoke from little adobe chimneys and crooked stove pipes. I see a black-haired woman open a second floor door and toss a pan of water over the brown earth wall to the dirt beneath. I see a turquoise blanketed man climb down a third floor ladder and walk to the rear of the second floor roof, disappearing over its back wall.

The Plaza is quiet. Neither trucks nor cars enter or leave. An occasional man, wrapped in a multi-colored blanket from head to foot against the chilly January wind, comes to the river to fill a bucket or walk over the wide wood planks crossing the water to the other side. They take no notice of me.

I walked the length of the Plaza to the low adobe wall marking the eastern boundary. I turned around and looked out west and saw how the earth rose from the Taos Valley floor to the flat, hard packed dirt of the Plaza and then higher, behind me, into sensuously rounded mounds, heaving up to their pine-covered mountain peak.

I sat on the adobe wall in the quiet of the late winter afternoon. Directly across the Plaza from me was the small Catholic Church, San Geronimo, marking the end of the Native Americans' time alone, and the beginning of the clash of cultures, of the forging of something new.

This land is more than a geographical place on a world map. It is more than its earth forms and climate. It is an integral part of the organic life of men and women born and developing here.

The word Taos is a sixteenth century Spanish approximation of the Tewa word for dwelling. The Native Americans dwell here. They do not simply exist or live, use and move on. They dwell here. They are the land upon which they walk, the horizon they scan, the deer they hunt, the water they capture from the sky.

The land has become a Native American Pueblo. Arising out of this conscious encounter is the spirit of the place which informs each new member of the tribe who he is, who she is, as dutifully and clearly as their parents or their Kiva training.

Neither born nor reared here, the spirit of this place will never fully reveal itself to me. I do not belong to it. It does not belong to me. But I can come here as a pilgrim, aware of its presence, and listen. It will have something to say to me. Today it speaks of dwelling.

I was sad when I thought of an old saying around here. *The Native American sees the Spanish as nomads. The white man he does not see at all.* I remembered once a man from the Pueblo told me that when he looked at the feet of white people, he saw car wheels.

Long ago, the Native Americans called their village Ialaphai which means "place of red willows." I looked along the banks of the Río Pueblo, and saw those slim willow trees. Into how many storms have they bent, yielding for the moment, then curving back in the warm aftermath? Into how many baskets have their pliant branches been woven? The red willow, rooted yet flexible.

It was a long walk back to town and already the western horizon had begun to bleed into streaks of turquoise and orange. Walking back, the wondering begins.

How had this miniscule Taos Pueblo survived surrounded by the loudest, most powerful culture in the world? We flung our McDonalds and Holiday Inns around the world. We slapped our technology, our language, our values, on one country after another, whether they wanted them or not.

Taos Pueblo has survived, and I can learn from its people how to survive my own battle against materialism, financial pressures, and fear. I can learn how to be faithful to myself.

Survival has something to do with the delicate balance of the rootedness and flexibility of the willow. With patience. With humility before the rising sun, thanksgiving before a piece of bread. It has to do with veneration of the old and listening to the new. It may even have something to do with dying in order to survive with honor.

OCHO

Substitute Teacher — Really

After going through seven jobs in my first eight months in Taos, I finally had a foot in my profession and after a week of patient, hopeful waiting, the phone never stopped ringing.

"Miss Naylor, this is Lorenzo Montoya over at the high school. Can you come teach senior English today?"

"Good morning, Miss Naylor. This is Sammy Córdova. I need someone for third grade."

"Miss Naylor, do you want to work today? The Special Education classes at the Middle School. You'll have to start with hall duty at eight o'clock a.m."

"Catherine, Lorenzo here. Can you come in again? Junior social studies. Sure would appreciate it."

I met the principals who handed out the jobs: David Blickenderfer, Mario Barela, Eddie Abeyta, Herman Quintana. Subbing mostly in the Taos elementary school, I worked beside warm and wonderful teachers: Ana Cota, Betty Mullins, Stella Montoya and, of course, the Sister Act, the Clark grrrls from Arkansas, Anita Dominquez and Lavonia Hobbs.

But most of all, I met the kids. I called second grade roll: Abeyta. Barela. Martínez … . Little arms punched the air with: "Aquí estoy." "Aquí estoy." "Aquí estoy."

I caused a traffic jam in the junior high hall.

"Who are ya?"

"Who ya subbin' for?"

"Where ya from?"

"That your green truck out there?"

Gee, I thought, maybe they're hungry for someone who's not a Romero or a Martínez or a Córdova. Someone not "from here." Someone who wanted to share with them a different experience of growing up, of family life, of education, of lifestyle. Someone different who wanted to learn from them what it meant to be a kid growing up in Northern New Mexico.

During playground duty at the elementary school, I heard the jump rope calls, watched follow-the-leader. I saw the kids organize in two minutes for baseball and basketball games. Skipping, running, jumping. Jackets flying open. Shouts and screams.

"Teacher, can I help you after school?"

"Teacher, can you say my name?"

"Oh, teacher, will you be here tomorrow?"

Fifth-grade boys let me play basketball at lunch if I didn't mess up too much. Junior high kids demanded to know if that were my green Forest Service truck they saw through the window.

"Yeah."

"Do you drive it?"

"No, I have it towed everywhere I go."

Seniors asked where I was from.

"Chicago."

"Capone, uh? Cool."

"Well, there's Jane Addams, Studs Terkel, Sandra Cisneros."

"Who are they?"

"Sit down and I'll tell you."

I had forgotten about innocence and play. I had forgotten about the little child within me. Little Cathy, playing house in Mom's high heels and wearing her veiled and feathered hats. Little Cathy pretending that she rode a great Arabian horse named El Capitán as she ran through the prairies to school every day.

"Hey, Sammy," I called. "Throw me the ball. I bet I can make more free throws than you."

When the bell rang, I started my fifth grade class with a few minutes of meditation to calm them for an afternoon of work. During the last twenty minutes, I read them a story. Acting it all out. In seven voices!

That evening, at home, in my large one room, I turned on music. A friend had loaned me his old radio which got one local FM station. I dimmed the lights and danced. Different clothes. Different moods. Different styles. I was playing. I was growing young again.

One day, in ninth grade science, the students started the game "Get the Substitute." During the roll call I'd call a name and five voices would answer. I'd call someone who had dropped out a month ago and ten voices would answer. Pencils, spitballs, paper clips, paper airplanes polluted the classroom air. I wondered what London looked like during the Blitz.

"Okay, people. When your principal called this morning, he said something about teaching, but obviously that's not what happens here. So he can have you this period."

Twenty-nine voices beseeched me: "Don't call him! Don't call him."

"Nope, it's too late. Perhaps you won't learn science this period but you may learn something about being stuck with the consequences of your actions. We call it thinking before doing, being responsible for yourself."

So the principal came down and I salvaged the afternoon for skiing. A few weeks later I was called for that same seventh period science class. We learned some science that day.

In a senior world lit class, we went past the bell so intent were we on struggling to discover what myths we as a nation have established through the centuries to explain our values, our fears, our best hopes. Classes like this when you and the kids are excitedly walking on new ground, makes the tough job of substitute teacher worthwhile.

After a few weeks, the honeymoon was over.

Parents were circulating a petition to recall a Board member for all sorts of nefarious actions. Another parent group was outraged because Gideon bibles had been distributed throughout the schools. "What about separation of state and church?" they hollered.

The popular elementary school principal who kept me the busiest was being politically transferred to another school in exchange for its principal, but the parents over there got in an uproar and blocked the trade. All were questioning the firing of a female teacher.

The parents coalesce and reach critical mass, hired a lawyer, called up the news cameras from Albuquerque's television stations, made placards and T-shirts, staged a march and talked up a show down meeting with the Board. Many teachers weren't going to the meeting and warned me not to attend.

"Look, Catherine, I need this job. It's as simple as that."

"What do you mean, Lupita?"

"I mean if you attend that meeting and indicate that you oppose the Board's decision, you may get your name taken off the substitute list."

For a moment I felt fear, oppression. I'd only had this job for two weeks. I couldn't even think of risking being jobless again.

"Catherine, you're not in the big city schools here or moneyed, experimental private ones. This is Taos. Provincial, insular. The Board is made up of all men, all Hispanic men. You're a woman, an Anglo. Watch it!"

"You really think I could lose my job for signing petitions or speaking at that meeting?"

"Could be. You're quite dispensable. Why don't you just close your door and do your thing with the kids."

"Like an ostrich, uh?"

"Exactly. Why lose another good teacher?"

"I've got to get home and think about this. See you tomorrow."

I went home. It was nearly six o'clock and still light out. I sat on the swing in my yard, a slab of wood and two ropes hanging between an aspen and an apricot tree. A warm March wind moved me. Another week and it would be spring, the beginning of my fourth season in Taos.

I knew I had to attend that meeting. It was the right thing to do. I couldn't live with myself if I didn't. And, yeah, I'd have to take the consequences of it. And maybe the next morning I'll check in with Don Rael in the unemployment office. But what the heck! I clean a good toilet bowl. I was only staying for a year. Wasn't I? And only one season left.

The Sister Act waited outside my classroom at three p.m. on the day of the big meeting.

"We'll see you tonight," says Lavonia.

"We'll save you a seat," says Anita. They button up their coats, click their heels and disappear.

I asked myself again, how could I risk this job? How could I bear being out of work again? But my feisty Irish genes obliged me to go. I sat between Lavonia and Anita, who both spoke at the podium and then sat down, turned and glared at me until I got up and made a weak-kneed trek up the aisle. To this day I swear I heard whispers accompanying me on both sides: "Dead man walking. Dead man walking." I said what was on my mind, but I didn't make eye contact with the principals sitting in the front row who fed me my jobs. I figured if I didn't see them, they didn't see me.

Past midnight when the meeting finished, I staggered out to the sweet smell of spring creeping across the valley.

"Goodbye," I told the sisters. "I guess I'll go home and pack."

"Goodnight," they said as if nothing had happened. "See you tomorrow." A click of their heels and they were gone.

The next morning I start studying maps for escape routes out of town. It just wasn't working for me here in Taos. The sooner I called it quits, the sooner I could re-establish myself someplace else.

The phone rings. "Catherine," says David, "I need you in third grade."

"I'll be right over!"

As I'm dressing the phone rings again. It's Mario wanting me for sixth grade. "Oh, I'm sorry, Mario, David already called."

"Darn him. Well, next time."

I grab my things and gun my truck out of the driveway spraying gravel every which way. These are my kind of guys! This is my kind of town! And, what's more, I'm going to make it through to June. I've beaten the odds. I'm going to last a full year in Taos.

But first I gotta get to the kids. Remember the kids?

NUEVE

The Hostess

Once upon a time there were four gas stations at the entrance to Taos Plaza. Taoseños were going places in those days. When I arrived unannounced in June of 1977, only two remained, Texaco on the northeast corner and Chevron on the southeast corner. Phillips on the northwest corner had disappeared and John Nabours' Conoco on the southwest corner had just been gutted. Taoseños were no longer going any place. Now they had to stay home and mind the shops and restaurants they were building.

Ten men (nine too many) stood around Conoco's black hole and conjured up the Plaza Real. Shops downstairs and El Portal Comedor y Cantina upstairs. They coaxed the consummate restaurateurs Vern and Leota Matheny back to Taos to manage El Portal. The pair had a successful seventeen-year run across the Plaza at their famed La Cocina before selling it in 1970 to Cal Loving.

School was going to close soon so I applied for work at El Portal and was hired as a hostess. On opening night, May 25, 1978, against a backdrop of one of Nona Wesley's unique interior designs, which included the parrot Guido, hostesses Diana Schwab, Judy Gentry, Andrea Frost and I greet folks with our best black dresses and smiles. Ken "Shadow" Martínez, Kiva Harris, Rick Thady, Randy Raiser, Jean-Pierre Dhondt, mother and daughter Virginia and Charlotte Pérez, Tim Reed and Ralph Ayola kept the food and spirits flowing for the Taoseños and early summer tourists who streamed in to check things out. El Portal becomes The Spot for excellent food and a noon-to-seven happy hour with half-priced drinks, live music, and good times.

Matheny greeted each table with "Our house special is the Damiana Margarita, an aphrodisiac liqueur from a Mexican cactus. Would you like a half liter or a liter?" If someone asked if we served vegetarian meals, Matheny said, "Honey, if you're sick, go to the hospital." Over in the lounge Dennis Robbins, Jeff Bergerson, and John Vargas manned the bar. During the band's break we crowded the doorway to watch John Vargas jump up on stage and do his Elvis impersonation.

It was a great place to meet people. In fact, once I forgot I was paid help and actually went into the lounge, ordered a drink and settled down with a National Geographic Photographer on a shoot in Taos for a documentary on the New Mexican Pueblos. Luckily, a waitress coming into the lounge to pick up her drinks spotted me and came over.

"Hey, Catherine, didn't you just seat my table? Are you off already? Folks are standing round the desk.

There's no one there."

"Omigod!"

Drink in hand, I rushed back, black heels and all, to commandeer the desk. Placing the drink on the shelf beneath the counter, I didn't miss a beat.

"Good evening! How many?"

"Four."

"Fine. Right this way."

Back at the desk, I looked down at the glass of wine and wondered if I should be drinking on the job. I thought not and set the glass on the tray of the next waiter passing by. He raised an eyebrow. I shrugged my shoulders.

One Halloween night nearly shut us down. A full moon. A packed dining room. The lounge looked like a Star Wars convention. Then someone misspeaks and ka-BOOM! A barroom brawl exploded. Even the bartenders were in on it. Jumpin' Joe Cota turned up the volume on his keyboard and kept on jumping. Beer bottles and glasses flew overhead. A local lawyer, who may have instigated the fracas, cried "self defense!" with every punch he landed, "self defense!" with every chair he swung. Cocktail waitresses Jody Morgan and Ripple never missed a beat as they gracefully wove around the fists and bloody noses. The diners rushed toward the front door and spilled out into a moonlit night. "There go our tips," wailed the waitresses and waiters, who waded into the fray themselves. One diner with his

Stetson askew on his head and his napkin still tucked in his shirt asked on his way out, "M'am, y'all want me to come back with my rifle?"

Not long after that melee I got sacked. I couldn't remember the circumstances so about a year or so later I checked it with John Nabours, one of the El Portal owners, who was then enjoying running Radio Shack, an orderly operation.

"Well, first of all," he says, "you weren't known for your job stability."

"What?" I'm indignant.

"When I look at a resume with a month here and two months there, I'm thinking this one's a risk."

"You mean I was dumb enough to put that down?"

"Doesn't matter," John says. "I fired you because you were reading instead of seating the customers."

"But … ." I'm ready to defend myself when I hear my mother's voice: "Cathy, put down that book and come set the table." "Cathy, get your nose out of that book before you ruin your eyes." I see myself in my El Portal black cocktail dress with the spaghetti straps, one slipping down my left shoulder, sitting on a bar stool at the reception desk, my black heels dangling from my toes. I'm oblivious to the folks pooling in the lobby, politely coughing and shuffling their feet as I turn the pages of *Bless Me, Ultima*.

Reading is how I survived the empty afternoons sitting art galleries, the long nights at hotel front desks, the downtime at restaurants between the end of lunch and the beginning of dinner. I read to stay awake, to educate myself, to escape from these part-time, no benefits, minimum wage, union locked-out, dead-end jobs.

Should I become Secretary of Education I will see that no one is ever fired for reading on the job. Readers shall be given bonuses!

Within two years El Portal closed. *Por la gracia* I have survived over thirty-five years in the company of writers such as Rudolfo Anaya, N. Scott Momaday, John Nichols, Denise Chávez, Frank Waters. I ask you, esteemed reader, if not stable, am I not a survivor? And here in Taos, which virtue is more useful?

* * *

Having settled in Cañon within a week of arriving in Taos, I rented first a room in the San G on old Witt Road, later a stone's throw down the road María Benítez's dance studio, and then a small adobe on the back lot of Mary and Joe Sánchez's land. Most evenings found me at the Sánchez's kitchen table with other Taoseños drinking wine and shooting the breeze.

Some fourteen months later, restless for a new experience of Taos and just a few weeks prior to losing my job at El Portal, I had rented a small, three room adobe home in rural Arroyo Seco.

Within minutes I could be at Abe's Cantina to enjoy his green chile stew or up to the Ski Valley, not to ski, but to sit in beauty and have coffee with friends there or wind down the day driving down to Valdez to enjoy Happy Hour at The Bar. I made new friends in Seco: the painter Fritz Kackley, the computer whiz Johnny Archuleta, and painter and motor cyclist Ann Crombie.

DIEZ

Teacher — Almost!

One mid-November Sunday morning, I received a frantic call from a principal up north asking if I could bail him out of a crisis. His junior high kids had already run off their first two English teachers.

"I've heard good things about you from principals down in Taos. Could you come up today to get the books, sign the contract and start tomorrow? We'll pay you for your English master's degree and your seven years teaching in Chicago."

"Well, yes, I could come up to get the books to prep and be in class tomorrow. But let me see how the first week goes before I sign a contract."

"OK."

Such a deal! Best I had since arriving in Taos. Monday, I walked into the classroom with black boots, a denim skirt and a brightly colored sweater. I leveled with the kids. "Look. I'm trying this situation out. If I like what I see, I'll stay. If not, I'll take the week's paycheck and leave. And you'll be trying me out too. So on Friday, we'll all vote. Fair?"

They all nodded. I could see from their faces that they hadn't had time to develop their strategies to overturn the apple cart. So I moved in quickly. Being an experienced teacher, I knew that you start out strict and then loosen up—never the other way around.

I got to work with my classes: firm and funny, storyteller and listener, challenging and sympathetic, no nonsense and encouraging. To catch their attention, I used some "hells" and "damns" in the spirit of Shakespeare, who mixed-up the language of the groundlings and the upper crust and everybody in between in that creative crucible of the Globe Theater. I'd say something like, "Even if you don't give a damn about your education, I do!" The kids didn't know whether to smile or gasp.

It worked. It all worked. Plus, I couldn't hide my absolute joy about being in a classroom again. Teaching in Chicago schools in the '60s was as good as it gets. Think of your best ideas for improving education and back then we probably had them up and running. It was a golden age of innovation, collaboration, autonomy and hope. We teachers weren't filling vessels. We were growing flowers. Looking at these kids I saw bright daffodils, wild sunflowers, quiet violets, morning glories and a couple of thorny roses. I loved them all.

The week flew by and on Friday I told each class that I wanted to be their teacher. Did they want me for a teacher? Applause and yeas all around. It was a deal. I'd be their teacher for the rest of the year.

I flew down to the principal's office to sign the

contract. Thrilled! I had a real job in Taos. At least in Taos county. Life was good.

"I'm sorry it didn't work out."

"What do you mean? I'm here to sign the contract."

"One of our Board members is a minister and when he heard about the swear words, he demanded that we let you go. I'll pay you for the week according to the terms I promised."

Pow! I sat down and when I could breathe again, I asked if I could meet with the Board member to explain myself, meet with the whole Board, have them observe my classes. I'm almost ready to offer to clean their houses and do their laundry. I told him that I had done what he had asked me to do: Get the kids to settle down and learn. On Sunday the guy was on his knees begging me to take on his hellions, on Friday I was on my knees begging to keep them. I wanted to strangle him, but clearly it was his job or mine. There was no attempt to work it out.

"You don't have to come back for your check. I'll mail it."

"Oh, yes, I'll come back." I stood up. "I'll come back Monday and tell each class what happened. I don't want them to think I betrayed them. That I didn't want to be their teacher. And don't you dare try to stop me."

I marched out and slammed the door so hard I covered my head waiting for the walls to fall. I cried so hard driving back to Taos I put on the windshield wipers, thinking it was a rainy day.

As my mother always said, "Sometimes you can't win for losing." So there went my ninth job in fifteen months, for an average of one job every 1.67 of a month.

That weekend neighbors' and friends' advice ranged from "Sue the bastards" to "You should have known better. You forgot where you were."

Right. I wasn't in the Chicago schools where principals told superintendents to lay off the teachers so that they can get their work done. Where a superintendent tells a complaining Board to "shadup and sit down or go teach the damn kids youseselves." No, I was no longer in that rough and tumble City of the Big Shoulders.

I was in a village of soft adobes and subtle ways. I was in a school system that protected and passed down its people's culture and I had been plucked out of its throat like a stuck cough drop. Utterly disposable. For if I could use swear words in class, what else was I capable of?

Monday, I told the young, gangly Anglo fellow who sat at the teacher's desk that I'd like to talk briefly to each class. "Yes," he murmured and continued sitting at his desk. Teary eyed, I explained to the students what had happened and apologized if I had offended them with my language. "Oh, Miss, we say worse on the playground!" Doesn't matter I told them. The guys called out, "Tell us who squealed. We'll take care of it. We'll getcha back." I told them to work hard, to graduate from high school and to go on to college.

After the last class, I walked over to the Board member's house, just down the block. His son hadn't been in school. I knocked on the door and the boy answered. "Oh, Miss," he cried, "I didn't mean for my dad to tell. The kids will hate me." I walked in and sat down and motioned for him to sit down. I reached over and took his hands in mine. "They don't know. Besides it's not your fault. It's mine. Get back to school tomorrow. Tell the kids you had the twenty-four hour flu."

I grieved that beautiful dream that had slipped through my fingers. I wondered about my chances of making a good living, a good life in Taos and wondered if I should move to a city where I could get a full-time teaching position and grow a career. I had just lost my ninth job in fifteen months but I thought of the Taoseños who couldn't pick up and leave as I could. They weren't here for the summer or just for a year or two. They had kids to feed and clothe, and elders to care for. In every way, I was an outsider.

I stood for hours at a western window in my little rented adobe in Arroyo Seco, where, looking out, my spirit could stretch across the Río Grande, across the mesas, across Arizona and California, out to the Pacific. I remembered being a teenager in the '50s when "White flight" gripped Chicago's South Side. Blacks were crossing the borders of their enforced ghettos and coming into the all-White neighborhoods and in turn the Whites were either rioting or scrambling further south. Change was frightening. Fear of the intruders had poisoned the air.

Now, some twenty years later, the tables were turned and I was the intruder with different ways, a troublesome challenger. The quieter I grew, standing at that window, the clearer I could hear that still, small voice within. Stay, it said. Stay. You know how to leave. Learn how to stay. Experience being the outsider. It will open your heart. It will teach you compassion.

I soon realized that not getting that teaching job was neither here nor there. I would let myself become something else ... if not a teacher ... something else ... something better. I needed to believe that I was of that immense universe outside my window and that still small voice within was my North Star. It told me to stay, stay in Taos.

Is this when I made the decision that Taos is home and decided to stay or did I make a decision not to cave and to prove to myself that I could find another job and in that victory stay a little longer?

ONCE

The Waitress

The next day I drove up to the Taos Ski Valley and got hired as a waitress at the St. Bernard Hotel.

That night my sister Mary called from Chicago. Mom had been rushed to the hospital with symptoms of a possible heart attack.

I called the St. Bernard and then booked a flight on Southwest from Albuquerque to Chicago's Midway airport, where I would rent a car and drive up to Mom's condo. How would I explain to the Godfathers that I had quit a job before I had even started? I had lost two jobs in two weeks, fourteen jobs in seventeen-and-a-half-months. Would they quit on me?

There had been no heart attack. Mom was fine. We had a great visit. Then back to Taos. Back to frozen pipes, a flooded floor and no job.

1979

"The most exciting discoveries happen at the frontiers. When you come to know something new, you come closer to yourself and to the world."

— John O'Donohue, "Eternal Echos: Celtic Reflections On Our Yearning to Belong"

DOCE

Office Manager

Refusing to give up and not clear why I'm staying and despite Mom's admonishment during our Saturday afternoon phone calls, "Cathy, get your feet on the ground," I check in with my pals Phil Rivera at the Labor Department and John Holland at his Plaza drugstore, matchmakers of the Taos job market.

Rivera sends me over to Rivera. What to make of that? Henry is in need of a manager to run his Prudential Insurance office in Piñon Plaza. I'm hired during my interview with Henry and start the next day. On Friday I'm invited to his home to have dinner with his family. His wife Judy serves pepper steak, which I'd never had before, and enjoyed it. She sends me home with the recipe.

I think maybe now I'm going to make it here in Taos!

Henry's a quiet guy and a hard worker. He never sits and chats with me, never asks any questions about my life, how I'm doing, what my hobbies are. When he's in the office, he plays soft Christian music. The minute he leaves, Bill Sarson, who rents desk space from Henry, and I run to the radio and switch the station. If Bill gets there first, it's KKIT country; if I win, it's KUNM jazz. Then Bill starts his daily repertoire of jokes. He's a self-employed appraiser and as warm hearted and funny as they come. When we spot Henry's car pulling into his parking space out front, I switch the station back to the harps. "As you were," I quip to Bill as I pass by his desk.

I have two other reprieves from the heavenly music and the incessant insurance claims: Deckerhoff's Stationery and Printing, and the Chicago Deli. Deckerhoff's is right next door and I bounce in a couple of times a day for paper clips or pencils to flee the angelic choirs and to pick up town news and chat with fashion maven Elva Padilla Archuleta. I'm a regular at the Deli on the other side of Deckerhoff's. A Vienna hot dog and the lunch crowd camaraderie fortify me for an afternoon of the waters of salvation and the everlasting claims.

"I lost my dog. Was he insured with the house?"

"I think I hear the gophers at night tunneling under my floorboards. Are they an act of God? Will Prudential pay to fumigate them? If not, my whole house will fall down and then The Rock will really have to cough up!"

"I never got a notice last year that my policy was about to run out. Please renew it from the day before it ran out." Then, of course, the story of the robbery last week comes out.

After a number of months, the office just didn't feel right. I was too much of a people person to spend forty hours a week with a quiet boss and that quiet music. Bill told me he was surprised I stayed as long as I did and that he would miss me.

Nevertheless, while I had been doing time in the labor camps of the '70s, I fulfilled the requirements of becoming a naturalized citizen of Taos County: I established permanent rental residency; I exhibited an eccentric character; I existed below the national poverty line. I just didn't know to whom or to what to swear allegiance. The King of Spain? The Taos Mountain Casino? Manby's Ghost? La Llorona's Ghost, who eerily weeps at night along the creeks of Taos for her lost children?

Would somebody please tell me before my hard-earned citizenship is revoked. I sure would hate to be kicked out of Taos County on a technicality so late in the game.

TRECE

Gallery Sitter

If I can make it in Taos, I'll make it anywhere. New York stole those lyrics from us. I think Don Severino Martínez in his hacienda period here in Taos in the early 1880s wrote them or was it our beloved painter from Navajo country, R. C. Gorman? Either way, if Liza Minnelli and Frank Sinatra had ever done time here, even for a day, they would have known that song had the Taos brand all over it.

I made it here in '77 and '78, and in '79 I was still making it. Sort of. It was the season of joblets. Two of them were on Kit Carson Road, one glamorous, one bizarre, and another, believe it or not, was in Texas.

The Julia Black Gallery at 119 Kit Carson Road stood for elegance, bold artists, rave openings, back room champagne deal closings and stunning assistants like Mary Alice Merritt and me. Julia Black had the glamour! A statuesque blond who could have been modeling in Paris, she was mothering two girls, keeping an art gallery out front and afloat, and gracing us all with her high spirits and jinks. What fun the three of us had until she up and married one of her artists and followed him to Ashland, North Carolina.

CATORCE

The Gardener

I was hired further up Kit Carson Road by Belford "Paco" Blackman as part of his dream team to reopen the Leon Gaspard house as a museum and designated historical site. Gaspard, a Russian émigré and internationally known painter like Nicholai Fechin, settled in Taos in 1919. The house was filled with his vibrant, colorful paintings and a multitude of artifacts that he and his first wife Evelyn brought back from their world journeys. Frank Water's book, *Leon Gaspard*, catches glimpses of this hugely spirited man and artist. After his death in 1964, his second wife Dora Kaminsky, also a well-known artist, married Paco Blackman and when she died in 1977, Paco was lord of the Byzantine pink mansion in Cañon. So much for the lineage of the estate keys.

The enigmatic Paco fantasized a European country house out there under the cottonwoods. I was the peasant on tulip detail. I planted five-hundred and fifty-eight bulbs. On my knees. Standing up, I fed the burros and Paco's pet Araucana chickens that astonished us with their green eggs. Others cared for the sheep, the cornfields and the vegetable plots. I also helped fix lunch for all those bucolic workers around the manor. Most were from the Pueblo, who never let on that they were watching one more circus come to town, knowing it would blow away like tumbleweed, which it did. It's a private residence now, but still with the fabled sign: Leon Gaspard 1882-1964, GASPARD HOUSE MUSUEM, Old Mansion of the Famous Russian-American Painter.

The best part was having a seat for supper at the long dining room table. Menus from around the world and the most remarkable guests appeared nightly. Some evenings, after supper, we'd all traipse down to the Taos Inn. Rámon Hernández, perched like an Hispanic leprechaun on his stool in the small, cozy bar, would be strumming his guitar and singing requests.

Paco sang like one of the Gypsy Kings and magic happened the nights that attorney Joe Caldwell and accountant Marty Martínez stopped in after work with their guitars. We'd go on until last call. Early the next morning, even before the sun started blazing its way across our New Mexican blue sky, I'd be on my knees again with a Triumph tulip bulb in my left hand and a trowel in my right. That summer I was convinced I had chased a white rabbit down a hole.

QUINCE

Kelly Girl

When the garden work ended, my cat Nova and I took off in my pickup for Houston to stay with my sister Pat who, along with five children, had followed her corporate husband Warren from Chicago's South Side, where we all had been born, to steamy, youthful, booming Houston. My plan was to make some quick money as a Kelly Girl to fund Spanish lessons at Cuauhnahuac, Instituto Colectivo de Lengua y Cultura in Cuernavaca, Morelos, Mexico. I hoped speaking Spanish would allow me to grow tall like Alice and throw off the curse of the Taos Bad Job syndrome.

The next morning I'm in downtown Houston filling out a job application and checking every box under "Skills." People looking for work are the same the world over. We can do anything. The following day I have six offers of temporary office jobs. Before long I'm making enough money to actually count and stack it on Pat's kitchen table. Warren, of course, is driving his money home by the truckload. No matter. Soon I'll be flying down to Mexico.

Pero quando yo vuelvo, voy hablar en Español! Start spreadin' the word.

1980

"We shall not cease from exploration
And the end of all our exploring
Will be to arrive where we started
And know the place for the first time."
— T. S. Eliot, "The Four Quartets"

DIECISÉIS

The ESL Teacher

Strange, isn't it, that I travel down to Old Mexico to learn Spanish in order to reenter New Mexico as an unbeatable job *candidato*? I know those old friars and conquistadors were chased down to El Paso in 1680 by the Native Americans and then crept back up in 1692, when things had simmered down. Since then many other folks have gone and come back. No doubt the cool Pueblo folks were the only ones who got it right the first time.

There I was, in the summer of 1980, in Cuernavaca, "City of Eternal Spring," strolling the *avenidas* perfumed by the showy bougainvillea, its small white flowers surrounded by magenta leaves; browsing in the *mercados* aswirl in bright colors, jubilant voices and intoxicating smells; climbing the Xochicalco pyramids; sipping coffee late in the evening in the outdoor restaurants of the great Plazas with hundreds of gregarious Mexicans. I came to the language school a week early to get my bearings and was strictly on tourist patrol.

On my first day at Escuela Normal Superior del Estado de Morelos, I left my rented room, where the shower's hot water turned off after fifty-nine seconds, stuffed my backpack with toilet paper, took an over-the-counter pill laced with opium so my stomach didn't turn itself inside out and hopped on a bus.

When I arrived at the school and registered, Lupe, the registrar, found out I had a master's degree in English. She jumped up and cried out to me, "Our English language teacher just cancelled. We need one. Now!"

"But I'm here to learn Spanish," I protested.

"English first," she commanded, "then Spanish." She turned her desk sign around from *Abierto* to *Cerrado* and turned me from *una estudiante* to *una maestra*. In an instant. No questions asked. She dragged me like a prized captive to the director's office, her long hair flapping like a black flag against her blouse of oranges and reds.

"We have an English teacher for tomorrow," she announced triumphantly. "Americana. Catalina Naylor."

"Qué bueno! Wonderful!" A tall, slim man dressed

in white pants and a white shirt reached over his massive desk to shake my hand.

"But ... ." I wanted to tell whoever would listen that I only wanted to be a student. I only wanted to be there for three weeks. No one listened.

"Lupe," he said, "Get Catalina's work papers in order. Explain the pay, procedures, all that." Then he turned to me again, smiling warmly.

"Bueno, Catalina. You start tomorrow at eight. It is our honor to have you."

Honor? A boss says to me that it's an honor to have me? I was seduced immediately and signed all the papers.

The next day I stood in front of a classroom facing thirty men and women, Mexican high school English teachers, smiling up at me expectantly. Behind me, my desk was piled with their gifts of fruits and flowers. I burst out laughing, partly because the whole situation was so bizarre and partly because I was thrilled to have the adventure. But mostly because I had lost complete control over my life, especially my digestive system.

The second day, Laura, one of the students, invited me to stay with her. I thought, why not. Someone had to be in charge. Let it be Laura. She drove me to my rented room where I gathered up my few things and took me to her home replete with a private room for me, an elderly mother who cared for the house and made all the meals, and a husband I would have divorced in two seconds. We all got along, though, and living with them was a pleasure. They became my best teachers and kindest friends.

Each weekend other students invited me to their villages. The long bus ride was vintage Disney. Chickens and pigs and kids chased each other up and down the narrow aisle. The passenger next to me always had a billowing basket of fruits and vegetables that spilled out. For hours I sat with a lapful of apples and turnips and with a menacing rooster in the aisle looking at me cross-eyed. I dared not move. Who was in charge? Nobody.

After three weeks I finally became the student I had come there to be—with teachers who refused to say a word of English although they were fluent in the language. *"Español!"* they sang out. *"Solamente Español!"*

I remained with Laura's family and toward the end of my stay her mother nursed me through an illness of high fevers, aches, chills, and hallucinations. Every time I came to she was sitting by my side, rubbing me with alcohol, murmuring incantations and giving me potions to drink. There was no talk of doctors or hospitals. I thought, well, this would be where I die—Mexico. But this woman knew exactly what she was doing and after three days I rose up from the dead, speaking perfect Spanish. Should I ever be appointed Secretary of Health, my slogan would be: "A *curandera* in every household. The hell with health insurance!"

Soon it was time to make my *entrada* once again into Nuevo Mexico, scoot up El Camino Real, race north along the Río Grande and find, at long last, *buen trabajo en mi pueblo.*

This was my do or die effort, absolutely my last chance for a good job in Taos. If it didn't work out, I'd put on my gypsy boots and pack my bags.

DIECISIETE

Alcohol and Drug Counselor – Bingo!

The Taos County Alcohol and Drug Program opened in 1979 as a branch of the State of New Mexico's Mental Health Council. It was housed in the old La Tuatah motel off the Taos Plaza. I immediately went for an interview and was hired as a counselor. It was there that I started to climb up and down the Ladder of Success with my fellow workers: Charley "Sheriff" Martínez, Felix "Chum" Archuleta, Rámon "Batman" Trujillo, Ben Vigil, Antonio Córdova, Albina Tafoya, Arturo Ortiz, Joe Paul Concha, Teresa Duran Gonzales, Nova Martínez, Cindy Freeman Valerio, Rose Vigil, Max Madrid, Pat Suazo, Joe Márquez, Joann Lujan, Alex Coca, and Anna Martínez.

Did you ever throw a party and no one came? Well, that was us. The drunks hated us; AA despised us; the neighboring businesses thought we lowered their property value; the general public figured we were do-gooder nuts; the courts and probation officers were wary of us. But all that suspicion and resistance united us. Like fingers closing into a fist, we became *familia*. Dysfunctional, of course. But a family.

The state required a monthly client count to justify our funding so we counselors cruised through the demimonde of Taos checking the haunts of the street alcoholics and drug addicts. One place that always produced men who would get in our cars and come to the office with the promise of free cups of coffee was under the trees around the little bar in Valdez.

One day, returning from Valdez with two guys in the back seat of my car, one sucking on his wine bottle and the other hanging his head out the window, I heard my mother's voice clear as the wind whistling through that back window, "Cathy, what in the world are you doing?"

Not all the AA folks welcomed us onto their turf. They knew what they were talking about and for the most part, at first, we didn't. They worked out of their homes, in the cafés and on the phones; we had an office—so to speak. Each counselor was shoehorned into one of the old motel rooms with a bathroom but no phone. Our office manager, Rosie Valencia Suazo, had to step out of the front office in rain, snow, mud and wind, and yell down our dirt pathway, "Catherine, you're wanted in the lobby!" I'd step out of Room Three and yell back, "Be there in twenty minutes. I'm in a session." Passersby wondered if La Tuatah Motel had come back as a brothel.

The real sticking point between AA and us, I think, was that they were volunteers and we were paid—if you call minimum wage without benefits being paid. To me it's more like a tip with the salary missing. At any rate, to make peace I asked one of the venerable founders of the Taos AA to have a cup of coffee with me at Dori's Bakery and Café.

"Teach me," I challenge him.

"First of all," he says, "you have to know the Big Book."

"What's that?" I ask.

With an exasperated sigh, he picks up a book from the bench, raises it over his head and bangs it down on the table. Coffee, cream and sugar fly all over. "See," he bellows, "that's what I'm talking about! You don't even know about the AA bible. You're hopeless! All of you!"

After we wipe up our mess and assure Dori that nothing's wrong, we settle into the first of what would become weekly lessons. In no time at all, AA folks are running meetings in our Detox and we're taking our counseling clients to their open meetings at the Presbyterian Church by Kit Carson Park. I was so taken with the intimacy and fellowship of my first open meeting that I stopped in the supermarket on the way home to wander the booze aisles, contemplating developing a drinking problem so that I could belong to that group.

Sometimes it was hard telling staff from clients. We were all flawed, and most of us, from time to time, fell down on our knees, rolled the dice and implored Our

Lady of Luck to save us from ourselves.

One of the best memories for all of us was our world-renowned Christmas party. Clients and their families, staff and their families, all the lawyers and judges, all the school and agency folks with whom we worked, even tourists walking down the street, came early and stayed late. Traditional foods, like green chile stew, burritos, tacos; live music; colorful decorations; dancing. People were in every office and hallway, and especially in the Big Room. No alcohol and we still had a ball. Our motley crew had triumphed over suspicion, envy, skepticism, ignorance and fear. Why? Our food was good!

During my five year stint at that Program, I entered my most memorable event of hundreds of memorable events in my journal on February 6, 1980.

"I sat in my little office looking out the window watching the well-dressed, healthy looking, well fed, laughing tourists walking up Kit Carson with their packages and coffees-to-go. I asked myself for god's sake, why was I in the Santa Fe Pen last week?"

I was there because I had sought permission from our director to invite Louis Valdez, nationally known for his El Teatro Campesino, to teach us his method of spontaneously creating skits that would deal with our counseling situations. Both the counselors and their clients would dramatically be involved in each skit. I believed that this would be one more creative and helpful technique to use in our counseling program.

Valdez divided us into two groups. One counselor, Ann, and her volunteer counseling clients would work with local volunteer high school students, as approved by their principals.

I and my five volunteer counseling clients chose to work with Santa Fe Prison inmates. The prison agreed and we headed out to Santa Fe, where we had booked two nights in a motel: our arrival night and the next night after our prison work.

During that evening and the next morning each group spent time getting to know each other and discussing possible strategies. After lunch, we drove to our destinations.

Arriving at the prison, we went through quite a few steel-barred, locked and guarded doors bringing us deeper and deeper into the prison. Some of us began to second guess our choice, but it was too late. After the last door locked behind us, we were brought into a room with a large rectangular table and chairs.

The prisoners in their identical outfits were already there. They stood up and we all introduced ourselves. No doubt they were glad to get out of their cells for awhile. I explained to them the instructions and purpose of the Teatro. They were eager to begin.

In their skits several of the prisoners identified themselves as the judge, and appointed others to be the jury or family members or friends or a mixture of all three.

As judge or jury, the prisoners usually set themselves free. As family or friend, they pleaded with the judge or jury to pardon and set free their family member or friend. After each skit, the prisoner told the rest of us what they had learned from that exercise and received feedback from the others as to what they had experienced being part of the prisoner's skit. It was hard sometimes to hold back my tears.

It was late when we left the prison. We picked up food-to-go for supper and shared our day with each other in the Inn lobby. The school group had already dispersed and were up in their rooms. We soon followed and went to bed early eager to head home in the morning.

I got up early, as usual. Showered, dressed and started walking down the hall to the motel lobby where coffee and a breakfast would be laid out for us. I soon noticed, however, that there was a crowd in there and I, at five-feet-two, couldn't look over their heads to watch the television. I asked a man next to me what was going on. "There's been a riot in the prison here. It's still going on. Over thirty dead so far. Seems like the prisoners are in charge. Hope they don't come over here."

I sat down afraid I would fall. I couldn't take it in. Did we cause this rampage with all those skits? How are the prisoners with whom we worked? Are they dead? Alive?

My fellow Program counselor, Ann, saw me. She rushed over, pulled up a chair and reached for my hands.

"Catherine, I'm so sorry. This is unbelievable. And scary. We and the kids better stay here until things calm down. Can I get you coffee and some coffee cake?"

"No. Yes. Oh, I don't know."

"Just sit here, Catherine. I'll get you something to eat."

"Thanks, Ann."

The motel's front desk person came over and told us that some parents have called. "I gave them the latest news. They said that they wanted to speak to their kids to tell them to stay put because they were coming down from Taos to pick them up."

"Sure. Fine. The rest will drive back with Ann and me."

All I can remember about the rest of the day is that all we Taoseños got home safely. The next day I read the newspapers: "a thirty-six-hour riot," "thirty-three inmates lost their lives," "one-thirty p.m. Sunday the police and National Guardsmen retook the penitentiary."

For weeks afterwards, I called the Santa Fe Police Department and the Prison, read off the names of the prisoners I had worked with wanting to know if they were all right. The response was always the same: "We're not at liberty to discuss this case." In my last phone call, knowing that I had to give up, I told the policman who answered who I was and why I was calling. I asked him if he thought our work may have caused the outbreak. "Oh, no," he said. "This had been brewing for weeks."

* * *

That brave new and strange world became *mi vida loca* for five magical years, 1980-1985, after which I left for Chicago for two years to earn a master degree in Counseling Psychology at the Alfred Adler School of Professional Counseling Psychology. I wanted to be the best counselor I could be. During that time, I was hired by Arthur Andersen, a prestigious Chicago accounting firm. I worked with its consulting side. It offered good money, great co-workers and traveling the country to teach new consultants the skills of public speaking and team building.

During those two years in Chicago, it was never a question but that, with degree in hand, I would return to Taos to set up my private counseling practice, which I did from 1987-1995, while continuing to fly the friendly skies of Southwest Airlines for Arthur Andersen until 2001, when I retired.

DIECIOCHO

Writer and Assistant Editor

In September of 1999, a Taoseño named Bill Whaley was publishing *Horse Fly*, a free monthly newspaper. I loved it! Bill's writing, whether a discussion of local politics or a critique of the arts, was a course on the history and heart of Taos. His paper also had regular and guest columnists, illustrations that nailed their topic, and, of course, ads that kept the paper free. In February of 2000 I sent in a column, which turned into monthly columns. I advanced to copy editor and assistant editor.

Bill was the best boss I ever had. He told you what he needed and left you to follow through. There was no checking in every fifteen minutes to look over your shoulder to see how you were doing. Being trusted brought out the best in us. Bill will always be Boss Whaley to me.

In September of 2009, Bill bid his *Horse Fly* adieu. I still miss it and from time to time, I'll sit down with a cup of coffee and reread my souvenir copies.

EPILOGUE

During those Taos years there were lots of forks in the road, lots of wrong turns and doubts, and lots of wrestling matches with a dusty village jealously guarded by Taos Mountain, which natives said had the authority to let you stay or spit you out, and all overseen by the bluest of blue skies.

But this outsider, this Gypsy girl belonged in Taos with the Pueblo Native Americans, the Hispanics, and the Anglo adventurers. She belonged with the dirt roads, the hills, the rivers, the coyotes and mountain blue birds, her favorite coffee shops and watering holes, the soft sunrises and flaming sunsets.

Catherine and Taos were in each other's memories now, a photo in one another's album, forever in the same story. She was home. A home that one job after another had built. Taos had become her treasure in the field. Her pearl of great price.

Author
Catherine Naylor

I was born and raised in Chicago, "City of the Big Shoulders."

By age three I was able to climb up on a chair and reach a painting by my namesake, my grandmother Kate Leahy Naylor. It was of a Gypsy boy. It took years to shed all other identities except that one and begin my wandering. I went to Ireland to visit my relatives, up and down the States to get to know America, and further down to Australia to get to know myself.

So it is I, who I am sure is the real Catherine Naylor, who wrote this book. I hope it is as much of a joy for you to read as it was for me to write.

* * *

When I was a second grader at St. Clotilde Grammar School on Chicago's South Side, a seemingly ordinary incident happened, whose consequence would not appear for another thirty-years.

One morning our teacher told the students in the row by the black board that they were now third graders. I was in that row. We didn't know if our second grade was overcrowded and we just got passed on, or if we were smart kids, or dumb kids who needed help from a more experienced teacher, or for that matter were trouble makers our teacher wanted to get rid of.

Nonetheless, when a nun spoke—it was papal doctrine. No questions asked. That's the way it worked back in the 1940s on Chicago's South Side. But as the years rolled on, I reckoned that Life had pushed me ahead of myself and I wanted that time back to catch up.

An opportunity came when I arrived in Santa Cruz, California in 1976. I found a job ad in the Santa Cruz Sentinel looking for someone to be a "presence" during the fall-to-spring off season at Kennolyn Camp, a summer camp for kids, high in the redwoods of the Santa Cruz Mountains. I interviewed with Max and Marion Caldwell and was hired. I couldn't have had friendlier bosses than the two of them.

I lived rent-free in a large, comfy cabin, doing light office work, mainly returning phone calls and sending out brochures, and even lighter housekeeping in the Caldwell's beautiful home overlooking the Monterrey Bay for which I was paid.

In no time at all, I claimed this time as that lost year of my childhood. I named it "My Henry David Thoreau

Year." I hiked the hills, explored the ravines, read and wrote in my journal on the cabin's porch. Several days a week, I'd walk four miles through the Soquel Woods down Glenn Haven Road to Caffe Pergolesi in the heart of downtown Santa Cruz. It was there that I met Louise White, a high school teacher, who invited me to join her writing group, which met weekly at the Caffe.

Thanks to Louise for handing me Howard Zinn's book *People's History of the United States, 1492 - Present,* and for our summer trip visiting Native American homelands which led me to Taos, New Mexico, which would be my soul's home for more than thirty-seven years.

www.ingramcontent.com/pod-product-compliance
Lightning Source LLC
Chambersburg PA
CBHW030049100426
42734CB00038B/945